# The Longhaired Cat

Grace Pond *and* Muriel Calder

**B. T. BATSFORD LTD** London

First published 1974

© Grace Pond and Muriel Calder

0 7134 2823 6

Printed in Great Britain
by Willmer Brothers Limited, Birkenhead
*for the publishers*
B. T. Batsford Ltd, 4 Fitzhardinge Street, London WIH 0AH

# The Longhaired Cat

# Contents

# The Illustrations

## Line Illustrations

The Author and Publishers wish to thank the following for permission to reproduce the illustrations appearing in this book: John Alexander Studio for fig. 11; Anne Cumbers for figs. 1–10, 12–15, 17–31 and 33; Peter Dance for fig 32; Sheila Harrison for figs. 34–41; Photos Serafino for fig. 16.

# Chapter one

# Introduction

## Origins

Of all the domestic animals the one familiar to more people throughout the world than any other is surely the cat but strangely enough very little is known as to its beginnings. Loved by many, regarded as a nuisance by some, and even with horror by others, thousands of words have been written about the *Felis catus* endeavouring to trace its origin and history but much is still surmise.

From Egypt more than 4,000 years ago comes the first definite evidence of domestication. There the cat was worshipped as a god, featured in frescoes and statuettes and embalmed on death but as far as can be seen those depicted always had short fur, long slim bodies and narrow heads. The Romans are said to have been responsible for introducing the first domestic cats to Britain but again these appear to have been short-coated.

Centuries later there came tales of cats with long coats in the East, in Asia, but no one knows how the length of coat originated or how long they had been in existence. At first, credit as a possible ancestor was given to the manul, or Pallas's cat, discovered by the traveller of that name in Tibet and Mongolia. It is still found there and occasionally may be seen in European zoos. The animal is about the same size as a domestic cat with thick longish fur, yellowish grey in colour. The head is broad, with small rounded ears set well on the sides and an unusual feature is the large eyes placed very high in the head, enabling the animal to peer over rock without being detected when hunting. Despite some similar characteristics, zoologists now consider the fundamental differences definitely preclude it as a

forbear. Credit has also been given in the past to the wild cat
(*Felis sylvestris*), which is approximately the same size and has
longish striped fur, brownish in colour but here again, because
of the broader skull and thicker blunter tail, this theory has
been ruled out now. However, it is known to interbreed with
the domestic cat and may have been responsible for some coat
markings.

The most probable explanation for the long fur is that it
started as a mutation among cats in a confined area and was
perpetuated through interbreeding, very much as must have
happened on the Isle of Man, where a mutation is believed to
have been responsible for producing cats without tails.

It was not until the sixteenth century that long-coated cats
were seen in Europe and some credit for these is given to a
learned writer, Nicholas-Claude Fabri de Peiresc, who was
said to have sent to Paris and other countries 'Ash-coloured,
Dun and speckled cats, beautiful to behold'. It is thought that
these cats came from Angora, later Ankara, in Turkey and they
were much admired and considered of great value. They had
long silky fur, but small heads, longish noses and large ears in
comparison with the long-coated cats of today. From Persia
came other cats with long fur, with broader heads, thicker and
longer fur, larger bodies and fluffier tails.

It is curious that although cats were so much admired and
were the subject of innumerable stories, poems, paintings and
sculptures throughout the years, that it was not until the nineteenth century that any interest was shown in the different
colours, markings and coat lengths and then very little was
written about this. In fact, when a Mr Charles H. Ross in 1868
told his friends that he was going to write a book all about cats,
they thought it most amusing.

His book is of great interest in that, in among the many
anecdotes and tales related, it must be one of the first to mention
the different varieties of that time—and this was before the
first official cat show. Of the longhairs he wrote

> The Cat of Angora is a very beautiful variety, with silvery
> hair of fine silken texture, generally longest on the neck, but
> also long on the tail. Some are yellowish, and others olive,
> approaching the colour of the lion; but they are all delicate
> creatures, and of gentle dispositions.

Writing on the Persian cat, he said .

> A variety with hair very long, and very silky, perhaps more
> so than the Cat of Angora; it is however differently coloured,
> being of a fine uniform grey on the upper part, with the
> texture of the fur as soft as silk, and the lustre glossy; the
> colour fades off on the lower parts of the sides and passes into
> white, or nearly so, on the belly. This is probably one of the
> most beautiful varieties and is said to be exceedingly gentle
> in his manners.

Dr Gordon Stables in *The Domestic Cat*, published in 1876, one
of the first cat books giving details of the different varieties,
referred to the longhairs as 'Asiatic Cats' and said that their
colourings and variety of markings were much the same as the
European or Western cats, the shorthaired. He wrote that 'The
heads of the white, blue and black ought to be small, round, and
sweet, the expression of the countenance being singularly
loving.' He went on to say that eye colour should be 'a blue eye
in a white Persian, a hazel in a black, and a lovely sea-green in
a tabby'.

As one of the earliest judges, he gave very useful rules as to
what to look for when judging the Asiatic (longhaired) cats.
These are well worth repeating:

> First scan your cats, remembering the difference in size you
> are to expect in tabbies from the other. Next see to the length
> and texture of the pelage, its glossiness, and its freedom from
> cinder holes, or the reverse. Then note the colour, and the
> evenness or unevenness of the markings. The head must be
> carefully noted, as to its size and shape, the colour of the
> eyes and nose, ditto the whiskers; mark, too, the lay of the
> ears and its aural tuft . . . lastly take a glance at the expres-
> sion of the face.

As well as referring to the angoras and Persians early writers
gave details of several other varieties with long fur which
appeared to have completely died out by the beginning of the
twentieth century, possibly through cross-breeding. John
Jennings, another early cat judge, as well as writing on the
angoras and Persians in 1893 wrote also on the French, Russian,
Chinese and Indian longhairs, which he said 'partake a great
deal of the Persian except that in India we have what is well

known as a "Tiger cat" with striped markings of red and black'. The French cats, he went on to say, were chiefly blue and had been bred in the first place by the Chartreuse monks. Strangely enough he does not refer to the 'pendulous ears' of the Chinese, surely a most unusual feature mentioned by other writers of that time. While most of these writers included the Chinese in the longhair varieties, there are references by others to the short black coats of the Chinese cats. His description of type is very much the same as that given by Gordon Stables but he comments on the fact that a number of the Persians' coats have 'an objectionable wiry tendency, getting also shorter, on the face particularly'. He blamed this on the result of shorthair crosses.

Harrison Weir, the organizer of the first official cat show in Britain in 1872, writing in 1889 set out standards, or 'Points of Excellence' as he called them, for the then known varieties, giving as colours for the longhairs white, black, blue, grey, red and any self colour; brown, blue, silver, light grey and white for tabbies. The head and body shapes were the same throughout for the longhairs but specific mention is made of the different fur texture and tail shapes required for the Persians, angoras and the Russians, proving that all three were in existence then. He wrote that the Persian's coat should be fine, silky and very soft; a slightly woolly texture in the angora and that this is more pronounced in the Russian. The tail of the Persian should be covered with long and silky hair throughout, somewhat longer at the base; the angora's is like the brush of a fox but longer in the hair; and the Russian equally long in hair but more full at the end, tail shorter, rather blunt like a tassel. For all varieties the head should be round and broad across and between the eyes, of medium size, nose rather short and dark at tip, ears ordinary size, but looking small, being surrounded with long hair, which should also be long on the forehead and lips. The standard regarding the type required was most far-seeing and depicted the longhair very much as it is today and far more modern in appearance than the examples of many cats photographed in the early days of the Cat Fancy, which had long noses and tall ears.

Although Harrison Weir was instrumental in organizing the first official cat show and was much gratified by its amazing success and that it proved to be the forerunner of many, not only in Britain but also throughout the world, he was most disappointed in that his first love, the shorthaired English (now known as British) cats became fewer in numbers due to the 'ascendancy of the foreign longhair'. This still holds good today with the number of longhairs exhibited rising all the time and in an even greater variety of colourings.

I feel it must be accepted that, because of a lack of understanding of breeding techniques, the early cats with different colourings and coat lengths were allowed to interbreed more or less indiscriminately: the more dominant characteristics prevailed until eventually the different varieties merged into one, which became the Persian. By then it probably differed considerably from the original cats from Persia. In fact, writing in 1903, Miss Frances Simpson, considered a leading authority of her day, and author of *The Book of the Cat*, published in 1903 by Cassells, said she had never been able to find out the difference between the angoras and Persians and preferred to consider the longhairs as Persians and the shorthairs as English and foreign cats.

At the first shows there were officially no such things as cats of pure breeding, as no records had been kept, and looking through old catalogues and stud books we find the parentage was given as 'unknown' more often than not. The majority of cats at the first show were short-coated, although there were classes for black, white, tabbies and any other colour angoras and Persians among others but, by the turn of the century, the numbers of longhairs had increased so rapidly that the proportion of long- to short-coated at the shows was said to be four to one.

In the beginning the Cat Fancy was almost the monopoly of the titled and wealthy, many of whom had servants who fed, groomed and generally looked after the cats, although the owners were frequently photographed holding an elegant longhaired prize-winner. It was, however, recognized that the lower classes could also own cats and show organizers put on special classes for working men and women with lower entry fees and smaller prizes.

In 1890, *Fur and Feather*, a weekly magazine (now fortnightly) dealing with small animals and birds, was started and articles on cats and reports of the cat shows began to appear. The National Cat Club had been founded in 1887, with Mr Harrison Weir as president and this club became the first registering body in the world to keep a list of pedigree cats, to 'determine the classification required, and to assist the showing and breeding of cats, by holding cat shows under the best sanitary conditions'.

North America became interested in the breeding and exhibiting of cats, many of which were imported from Britain, and several small shows were held. In 1895, Mr J. Hyde, an Englishman, organized a show at the Madison Square Gardens, New York, on similar lines to that of the National Cat Club shows at the Crystal Palace. No fewer than 176 cats were entered and, following this successful show, others were held at Boston and Chicago. These were the forerunners of many throughout the country and proved to be the foundation of the Cat Fancy in the United States.

Queen Victoria, who owned two blue Persians, and the Prince of Wales (later Edward vii), set the royal seal of approval on pedigree-cat breeding in Britain by attending shows and giving special prizes. Society was quick to follow their lead. Cats became fashionable and large catteries came into being. Lady Marcus Beresford was said to have had as many as 150 cats, so it is no wonder that her name was invariably among the prize-winners. When the National Cat Club was re-organized in 1898, the list of officials read like a page from Debrett, with HH Princess Victoria of Schleswig-Holstein as patron, Her Grace the Duchess of Bedford as president, and with the Right Hon. the Countess of Warwick, the Viscountess Maitland, the Marchioness of Dufferin and Ava, the Countess of Aberdeen heading the long list of vice-presidents. Louis Wain, the noted cat artist, was president of the committee, which included Lady Decies and Lady Alexander.

After disagreements, Lady Marcus Beresford started a second registering body, known as the Cat Club, in 1898 but this had a very short life and the National Cat Club reigned alone once more until 1910. By this time a number of other clubs had been started, although the National was still the registering body, but there were frequent dissensions, with the result that the National Cat Club agreed to relinquish all registering rights and the Governing Council of the Cat Fancy came into being, with the affiliated clubs having the right to elect delegates to represent them on the Council, with the National as the premier club having in perpetuity four delegates. The procedure is still the same today.

As the number of clubs and shows increased, so did the varieties and colours of the cats. By 1901 the longhairs recognized were black, white, blue, orange, cream, sable, smoke, tabby, spotted, chinchilla, tortoiseshell, bicolour and tricolour. The orange eventually became known as the red self, but the sables, spotted, bicolours and tricolours gradually disappeared. More recently the bicolours have been re-recognized and self browns or sables are again being bred but as yet have no official standard.

All the all-breed clubs were interested in the longhairs but at the beginning of the century their interests were looked after specifically by the Blue Persian Cat Society, the Silver and Smoke Cat Society, the Black and White Club, the Orange, Cream, Fawn and Tortoiseshell Society and the Chinchilla Cat Club. These clubs drew up standards for the respective varieties and suggested suitable persons as judges.

As there was no quarantine, it was quite easy to bring cats into Britain but usually the traffic was in the reverse direction: many an outstanding longhair went overseas for a high price to form the foundations of famous catteries whose pedigrees can still be traced back to their original British stock.

Chapter two

# The Longhairs:
# Standards, characteristics
# and varieties

The standard for the majority of cats with long fur is much the same generally speaking whatever the colour or coat pattern. There are certain exceptions for such as the Turkish, the Turkish angoras and the Birmans (see separate standards).

The heads should be massive and round, with good width between the small neat ears; the noses should be short and broad; the cheeks round and full; the eyes big and round and the chins firm. The bodies should be massive and cobby on short strong legs, with the tails short and full, not coming to a point at the end, and with no kinks. The coats should be long and flowing, with full ruffs forming a frame to the face.

Faults which may occur are: too long a body or tail; tall legs; small or deep-set eyes, large open ears, lack of chin, and over-shot or under-shot jaws.

One hundred points are allocated to the characteristics required in the standards recognized by the Governing Council of the Cat Fancy. These characteristics usually vary slightly with each variety, as some may be considered to be of more importance for one kind of cat than another.

The characteristics mentioned are those which would go to make up the perfect longhair—but such a cat has yet to be born. Some varieties, such as the blues and the whites, are perhaps nearer perfection than the others but most are improving all the time. Would-be exhibitors should not be disheartened if they feel their cats do not entirely fit the standards given, as even a top champion may fail slightly on some point or another. Although to a casual observer, a whole row of blue Persians, for example, may look identical at a show, to an experienced judge each cat differs in some way or another. Judges too may interpret the standard slightly differently, hence sometimes the variation in judging, with one judge putting up one cat as a winner and another judge a different cat.

## Self-coloured

Cats with coats the same colour all over are referred to as self-coloured in Britain and solid-coloured in North America. As far as can be ascertained, the first cats with long coats seen in Europe were self-coloured, often white, and cross-breeding eventually produced other colourings and coat patterns.

It was the self colours in the longhairs that were first given breed numbers in 1901, the colours then recognized being the blacks, whites, blues, orange, cream (once known as fawn) and sable. The orange eventually became the red self and the sable disappeared—and was therefore no longer recognized. Self browns and self lilacs are now bred but have not yet been recognized.

### BLACK

Looked on as a symbol of good luck in Britain and exactly the reverse in several other countries, black cats are considered by some as commonplace. Indeed there are many pet cats with short black fur but they are rarely entirely black, having white on them somewhere, and cannot be compared with the striking pedigree longhaired variety.

They are one of the oldest varieties recognized in Britain but yet still almost one of the rarest among the longhairs. They appeared in fairly large numbers at the early cat shows, and in the National Cat Club stud book for 1900 to 1905 (then the registering body) there were 15 males and 16 females entered but the numbers decreased steadily over the years and only recently—in Britain at least—has there been a notable increase. It is a different story in the United States where they have always been far more popular, although at the beginning of the century it was from Britain that many of the winning cats came.

The first blacks shown in about 1890 were exhibited by a well-known fancier of that time, the Hon. Mrs McLaren Morrison. They were Imp and Satan, who were said to have superb coats, and Satan was never beaten in all his long show life. Photographs of other blacks of that time show cats with more angora type, having big ears and long noses, but selective breeding over the years has resulted in animals of outstanding quality, frequently Best in Show. These have been produced by cross-breeding with other longhaired varieties, most frequently blue, and many a well-known champion has blue breeding somewhere in the pedigree. Outcrosses are still used to improve type. There is always the danger in a black/blue cross of the fur close to the skin having a slight blueish tinge. Whites have also been used most successfully, with excellent kittens resulting. A black may sire an outstanding white, and they may also be used as studs for the tortoiseshells, tortoiseshells and whites, smokes, creams and bicolours. Mated to a red they may produce tortoiseshells, although if the red has tabby markings, the kittens may have these too and once introduced such markings may prove difficult to breed out.

Striking in appearance, with jet-black fur and big deep-orange or copper eyes, the adults have many admirers but would-be owners are sometimes disappointed at the first sight of the kittens they hope to own. Although born black, in a few weeks the coat is apt to turn rusty brown, frequently with white or grey hairs appearing in the fur and it may be many months before the shining, jet-black coat is seen in its true beauty. However, it should be remembered that frequently the rustiest looking kitten in the litter turns out to be a glorious black when adult. As all kittens are born with blue eyes, it may be two or three months before they change completely to the deep-orange or copper colouring that contrasts so well with the jet-black coat.

Of all the longhairs, the blacks are probably the most difficult to keep looking immaculate and daily grooming is most important. The black fur reacts to damp and excessive licking and soon takes on a brownish hue, while if the cat is allowed to sit in the sun for long periods, the coat will very soon become bleached. Talcum powder should never be used in grooming as some is bound to be left in the fur looking rather like dandruff. Some fanciers do bath their blacks about a week before a show, allowing time for the natural grease to return to the coat but great care should be taken over the shampoo used—one safe for babies can be recommended. It is not necessary to bath at all and for daily grooming a few drops of bay rum, sprinkled well down into the roots, brushed well out and the coat then polished with a chamois leather or a silk handkerchief, will give a wonderful shine (see Grooming).

The type required for the blacks is as for other longhairs and because of the cross-breeding in the past, many are outstanding with good broad heads, small ears and big round eyes.

## STANDARD

### BLACK

*Colour*—Lustrous raven black to the roots and free from rustiness, shading, white hairs or markings of any kind.

*Coat*—Long and flowing on body, full frill, and brush which should be short and broad.

*Body*—Cobby and massive, without being coarse, with plenty of bone and substance, and low on the leg.

*Head*—Round and broad, with plenty of space between the ears, which should be small, neat, and well covered; short nose, full cheeks and broad muzzle. An undershot jaw shall be considered a defect.

*Eyes*—Large, round and wide open, copper or deep orange in colour, with no green rim.

N.B.—Black L.H. Kittens are often a very bad colour up to five or six months, their coats being grey or rusty in parts, and sometimes freely speckled with white hairs. Fanciers should not condemn them on this account if good in other respects, as these kittens frequently turn into the densest Blacks.

### SCALE OF POINTS

| | | | | | | |
|---|---|---|---|---|---|---:|
| Colour | .... | .... | .... | .... | .... | .... | 25 |
| Coat .... | .... | .... | .... | .... | .... | .... | 20 |
| Body .... | .... | .... | .... | .... | .... | .... | 20 |
| Head .... | .... | .... | .... | .... | .... | .... | 20 |
| Eyes .... | .... | .... | .... | .... | .... | .... | 15 |
| | | | | | Total | .... | 100 |

WHITES

History has it that the first cats with long fur, seen in Europe as long ago as the sixteenth century, were the whites, the original angoras which came from Turkey. Both in Italy and France they attracted much attention and when later they appeared in England were known as French cats.

These early whites had blue eyes and were thought by some to be dull and unresponsive, as at first it was not realized that frequently they were deaf. The coats were long and silky, the heads narrow, the ears upright and the noses long.

Cats from Persia were also brought to Europe. The fur too was long but the texture apparently differed from that of the angoras, being slightly more woolly and the colours were varied. They were heavier in build, with broader heads and smaller ears. Cross-breeding of the Persians and the angoras resulted in the type of the latter gradually vanishing until one writer and breeder at the beginning of the twentieth century wrote that she 'had never been able to obtain any definite information as to the difference between a Persian and an Angora cat'.

All these years later the wheel has now turned full circle and in the United States, the angoras, known as Turkish angoras, have been re-introduced direct from Turkey and are now being bred by several fanciers. Finer-boned cats than the Persians, their white fur is fine and silky, the heads are small to medium sized, tapering towards the chin and the ears are long and pointed; the tails too are long and tapering and it is quite easy to distinguish between the two varieties.

The element of deafness connected with the blue eyes still persists. There is thought to be some connection with albinism, although the white cats do not have the pink eyes seen in some white rabbits and in the human albinos. The early fanciers realized that this deafness factor existed and greater value was placed on cats with good hearing. Not all blue-eyed whites are deaf—the odd-eyed are occasionally, sometimes on the blue-eyed side, and the orange-eyed rarely so.

A little should be said here about the difficulties of owning a cat that is deaf. While it may not be possible to give the cat complete freedom particularly in a town with all the traffic problems, it is possible, if thought is given to it, for a cat to live almost a normal life. A garden can be completely fenced in or a large run provided for outside exercise but the cat can be allowed free run of the house. They will respond readily to vibrations and will come running when the floor is banged or tapped and also can be trained to answer to hand signals.

Affectionate cats, they love to be handled and nursed and at the shows will sit quietly in the pens, not affected by the noise but fascinated by all the activity around.

It was noted at the early shows that the cats with the bluest eyes often failed in type—that is, the noses tended to be too long—and various cross-matings were tried with blues, creams and black in an effort to remedy this. This was done most successfully but unfortunately the blue eye colouring was frequently lost, cats with orange eyes resulting. Cats with odd eyes, one blue and one orange, were also produced and eventually it was realized how important they were in future breeding, as they could produce both blue-eyed and orange-eyed stock.

For many years cats with both blue and orange eye colouring were exhibited in the same open classes at the shows and as those with orange eyes invariably won because of the better type, breeders considered it most unfair. In 1938 the Governing Council of the Cat Fancy had recognized the two varieties, giving both championship status. Even so, the blue-eyed cats gradually decreased in number and, up to a few years ago, only one or two appeared at the shows. More recently there has been a revival of interest and several breeders are now producing some excellent specimens.

In North America the blue-eyed whites have always been popular, doing well at the shows and frequently winning the highest awards.

It is difficult, when the kittens are young, to know always what the ultimate eye colouring will be. All kittens have blue eyes when they first open, the colour changing over the weeks. If the eyes are pale blue in colour then, they will rarely be a deep blue when adult. It is possible to pick out the odd-eyed quite early on, as there will be more density of colour in one eye than the other.

The whites with orange eyes—known as copper eyes in America—rapidly became very popular and over the years in Britain, America and on the Continent, have frequently taken the highest awards, including Best in Show. Outstanding in type, with big round eyes, they invariably attract attention wherever exhibited. Many are produced from pure white breeding but whites may also be produced from black/white matings, as well as blue/cream.

Odd-eyed whites appear in litters from matings of orange-eyed with blue-eyed, blue to blue-eyed, odd-eyed to odd-eyed, or odd-eyed with a blue- or orange-eyed. Frequently the type is outstanding and although they are recognized now in Britain, they have not yet been granted championship status. In North America they can become champions and one, Gr. C. Simbelair Aristocrat, was really outstanding, winning Best in Show a number of times when only just over a year old.

## STANDARD

### BLUE-EYED WHITE

*Colour*—Pure white, without mark or shade of any kind.

*Coat*—Long and flowing on body, full frill, and brush which should be short and broad; the coat should be close and soft and silky, not woolly in texture.

*Body*—Cobby and massive, without being coarse, with plenty of bone and substance, and low on the leg.

*Head*—Round and broad, with plenty of space between the ears, which should be small, neat and well covered; short nose, full cheeks and broad muzzle. An undershot jaw shall be considered a defect.

*Eyes*—Large, round and wide open, deep blue in colour.

### ORANGE-EYED WHITE

Description as for blue-eyed white except for eye-colour, which should be orange or copper.

### ODD-EYED WHITE

Description as for blue-eyed white except for eye-colour, which should be one eye deep blue and one eye orange or copper.

N.B.—Whites are very liable to get yellow stains on their tails from accumulated dust, etc. This very damaging peculiarity should be carefully attended to and stains removed before showing.

### SCALE OF POINTS

| | |
|---|---:|
| Colour | 25 |
| Coat | 20 |
| Body | 20 |
| Head | 20 |
| Eyes | 15 |
| Total | 100 |

Differing only in eye colour, the standards for the three varieties is the same, the fur to be pure white, long and flowing, and the type as for the other longhairs. Faults are any yellow stainings.

The kittens may have a pinkish appearance when first born but this soon changes as the fur grows and in a few weeks they are soon running around looking like miniature powder puffs.

Keeping a white looking immaculate may not be as difficult as it sounds. They appear to be very proud of their appearance and usually groom themselves frequently. The disadvantages are that the feet may become stained through walking on muddy ground, the fur beneath the tail slightly stained with urine and the tail, particularly that of a stud, be greasy and scurfy near the base (see Grooming). On the other hand, the fur is not so badly affected by the seasons, as is the case with the other self colours, such as the blue, which may become shady, or the black, which turns brown in the sun. Many breeders do bath their whites a few days before a show.

They are now used frequently in advertising both in the Press and on television and for this reason, perhaps, they are enjoying a small boom, with the kittens being constantly in demand.

BLUE

The blue longhair, or blue Persian, the name by which it is still called in many countries, is probably the most popular of all longhairs.

Unlike the blacks and whites, the blues did not have a class of their own at the early cat shows but appeared in the 'Any Other Variety' classes. Most blues had white on them in some form or another or had tabby markings. Eventually they were shown in the class for 'blue tabbies and blues with or without white' but, by 1889, things had improved and the class became 'blue—self-coloured'. This was so well supported that in the next year the adult classes were divided into male and female but the kittens had to be shown in the same class as the blacks and the whites.

At the end of the nineteenth century, Miss Frances Simpson, the writer, cat breeder and cat judge, did much to popularize the variety and her stud Beauty Boy was one of the first blue studs. In 1894, a male, Wooloomooloo, owned by a Mrs W. Hawkins, was said to be 'a grand blue'. He was responsible for a number of outstanding blue kittens and some modern cats have his name way back on their pedigrees.

Judging by the photographs of the winning blues of those days, although the coats were certainly blue, in other respects they little resembled the champions of today in that the heads were narrow, the ears big and the noses long. The fur was shaggy and regular grooming obviously could not have played such an important part in the care of the cat as it does today. Most of these blues had bright-green eyes and, although attempts were made to produce cats with yellow or orange eyes, it was said that many had eye colour of 'neither orange, nor yellow, nor green'.

In 1901 Miss Frances Simpson founded the Blue Persian Club which drew up a standard which was far-seeing and has scarcely altered at all since then and certainly gave the fanciers something to breed for. Gradually the eye colouring was improved, although some cats had eyes with green rims, a fault which still appears. Royalty, including Queen Victoria and HH the Princess Victoria of Schleswig, owned blues, and Society was quick to follow their lead, with the result that many more were bred. This meant that dedicated fanciers could choose the best from which to breed and eventually they became close to the set standard. The numbers went on increasing and they were the most popular pedigree variety until the Siamese took over much later on.

The improvement in type and coat continued and now nearly all the other self-coloured varieties owe their quality to cross-breeding with the blues way back. Indeed, as an example, at one time most of the champion blacks had a blue parent or grandparent. Blues were exported all over the world and many winning cats both on the Continent and in America have blues from Britain as their ancestors.

In Britain today the top blues are very close to the set standard, with beautiful, round, broad heads, well-developed cheeks and neat ears. Any shade of blue is allowed but it must be the same shade all over the coat and right down to the roots. Faults do appear in the form of white hairs in the fur; the eyes may be small or deep-set; the frill paler than the rest of the coat—all these would count against a cat being judged

1 An alert kitten with very sound black coat for his age

2 A White with odd-eyes having one a deep orange colour and the other blue

3 A Blue-eyed White with full coat beautifully groomed

4 A White from France with good orange eyes and type

5  A sturdy Blue in thoughtful mood

but a kink in the tail would count against it. The eyes tend to pale with age and the coat texture varies, perhaps, more so than other varieties. One cat will have fur that almost always looks beautiful, that rarely tangles or matts and requires comparatively little attention, while another's coat will knot up only an hour or two after grooming. Yet another's will be so soft that it will lie close to the skin, spoiling the appearance from a show point of view to the despair of the owner.

As previously mentioned, blues have been used to improve many other varieties and are mated to creams to produce blue-creams. Mated to a cream female, a blue male will sire blue-cream and cream males, while a blue female mated by a cream male may have blue-creams and blue males. A blue male mated to a blue-cream female may produce blue females, blue-cream females, blue males and cream males.

Like many other members of the feline family, the newly-born kittens may have quite distinct tabby markings. These

## STANDARD

### BLUE

*Coat*—Any shade of blue allowable, sound and even in colour; free from markings, shadings, or any white hairs. Fur long, thick and soft in texture. Frill full.

*Head*—Broad and round, with width between the ears. Face and nose short. Ears small and tufted, cheeks well developed.

*Eyes*—Deep orange or copper; large, round and full, without a trace of green.

*Body*—Cobby, and low on the legs.

*Tail*—Short and full, not tapering (a kink shall be considered a defect).

### SCALE OF POINTS

| | | | | | | | |
|---|---|---|---|---|---|---|---|
| Coat .... | .... | .... | .... | .... | .... | .... | 20 |
| Condition | .... | .... | .... | .... | .... | .... | 10 |
| Head .... | .... | .... | .... | .... | .... | .... | 25 |
| Eyes .... | .... | .... | .... | .... | .... | .... | 20 |
| Body .... | .... | .... | .... | .... | .... | .... | 15 |
| Tail .... | .... | .... | .... | .... | .... | .... | 10 |
| | | | | | Total | .... | 100 |

disappear as the fur grows and, by the time the kittens are a month old, should have disappeared. Once open, the eyes will be a bright blue but these gradually change and, although this may take a few months, should eventually become copper or a deep orange in colour. There are, of course, cats with too pale eyes and it has been found that frequently the deepest colouring goes with the darker blue fur—but this is not always the case.

Blues are most intelligent, love attention, are highly inquisitive and remain kitten-like in nature to the end of their days.

RED

This is one of the rarest of the longhaired varieties in that it is exceedingly difficult to breed such a cat with no tabby markings somewhere on the rich red fur.

In the early days of the Cat Fancy they were known as 'orange' rather than red, and according to the early show reports, were self-coloured with very few tabby markings but, as the classes were for 'orange, marked or unmarked', it is difficult to assess how good they really were. By 1910 they were referred to as 'red or orange', with separate classes being provided for 'red or orange tabbies' but by 1915, the term orange was no longer used. The colour had obviously deepened as the classes were now for 'red or shaded' and 'red tabbies'. Unfortunately little care was taken to breed only from the cats with the least markings, and eventually the selfs almost died out. White chins too were commonplace—a bad fault.

Of recent years there has been revived interest in the variety, with care being taken over the breeding, and many have taken prizes at the shows.

It is frequently said that all reds are males but this is true only when the mother is not pure-red bred. When both parents are of pure-red breeding, the resultant litter may well contain both male and female kittens. Reds are useful in the breeding of tortoiseshells and tortoiseshells and whites and, more recently, cameos. A black male mated to a tortoiseshell may produce reds and tortoiseshells.

As red selfs may appear in litters from red tabbies, it may not be apparent at first that a certain kitten is a self, as all the kittens will probably have some tabby markings at birth which may or may not eventually disappear and it is not until the full adult coat has grown, which may be at a year or eighteen months, that it is obviously a self.

The type is frequently good, with the head being broad and round, the nose short and broad and the big round eyes a deep copper colour. Faults are still tabby markings on the face and shadow rings on the tail.

## STANDARD

### RED

*Colour*—Deep rich red, without markings.

*Coat*—Long, dense and silky, tail short and flowing.

*Body*—Cobby and solid, short thick legs.

*Head*—Broad and round, small ears well set and well tufted, short broad nose, full round cheeks.

*Eyes*—Large and round, deep copper colour.

### SCALE OF POINTS

| | | | | | | | |
|---|---|---|---|---|---|---|---:|
| Coat .... | .... | .... | .... | .... | .... | .... | 50 |
| Body .... | .... | .... | .... | .... | .... | .... | 15 |
| Head .... | .... | .... | .... | .... | .... | .... | 20 |
| Eyes .... | .... | .... | .... | .... | .... | .... | 15 |
| | | | | | | Total .... | 100 |

CREAM

The cream is now a very popular variety but was once regarded as a sport, having in the first place appeared by accident from a mating between a blue and a red (then known as orange). Similar kittens appeared also in litters from tortoiseshells but the 'fawns', as they were then called, were considered 'spoiled oranges' and of little importance. They were usually neutered and became pets, although a few were sent to America where they were thought more of.

The first recorded 'fawn' was Cupid Bassanio in 1890 but it was said that his coat was patched and shaded. He does not appear to have sired as there is no record of his kittens. Eventually several fanciers did become interested in trying to breed them. They used red tabbies and tortoiseshells but, as mostly males were born and the few females produced appeared to be bad breeders, they did not get very far for a time. The early type was far from good; the ears were tall and the eyes almond-shaped. As tabbies had been used in the breeding, invariably there were bars and tabby markings, which proved difficult to breed out. In those days little was understood about the possibilities of crossbreeding and various matings were tried. Eventually it was realized that mating to blues produced the best results and later that it was possible to produce cream females and males to order, dependent on the colour of the stud and the queen. It is now a well-known fact that a cream female mated to a blue male may have cream male kittens and blue-cream female kittens in the litter; a cream male mated to a blue-cream female may have male and female cream kittens, blue male kittens and blue-cream kittens in the same litter.

The first blue-creams that resulted from these early experimental matings were usually referred to as blue tortoiseshells or blue and cream mixed and an early writer wrote of 'the risk of getting these oddities of half-blue and half-cream' from such matings. It was to be many years before the blue-creams, with their intermingled fur of blue and cream, were officially recognized, but the importance of the variety in helping to produce the beautiful creams of today should not be overlooked.

In the early days America was far more enthusiastic about the creams than England and a number were bought by Mrs Clinton Locke, a well-known cat breeder. One, a male, Kew Laddie, proved to be an excellent stud producing kittens of good colour. Today in North America, the cream has taken its place as one of the most popular varieties and has frequently won the highest awards at the shows.

Thanks to the efforts of fanciers in Britain over the years, the creams are now being bred very close to the recognized standard with good broad heads and big, round, deep-copper eyes. Faults are: that the coat may be 'hot'—that is, have a reddish tinge, particularly on the back—a white tip to tail; lightish fur underneath instead of being the same pure cream colouring all over; any bars or tabby markings.

Creams may also be used for mating to blacks, tortoiseshells, tortoiseshells and whites and, of course, to blues. Indeed as cream mated to cream indefinitely may mean a certain loss of type, an occasional blue outcross is recommended.

When selecting a kitten for future breeding, one with as few bars and markings as possible should be chosen.

## STANDARD

### CREAM

*Colour*—To be pure and sound throughout without shading, or markings, pale to medium.

*Coat*—Long, dense and silky, tail short and flowing.

*Body*—Cobby and solid, short thick legs.

*Head*—Broad and round, small ears well set and tufted, short broad nose, broad round cheeks.

*Eyes*—Large and round, deep copper colour.

### SCALE OF POINTS

| | |
|---|---:|
| Colour     .... .... .... .... .... .... | 30 |
| Coat and condition .... .... .... .... .... | 20 |
| Body .... .... .... .... .... .... .... | 15 |
| Head .... .... .... .... .... .... | 20 |
| Eyes .... .... .... .... .... .... | 15 |
| Total     .... | 100 |

## Tabbies

The first domestic cats known are said to have had tabby markings in some form or another and it is claimed that, if all the domestic cats in the world mated freely with one another, eventually all cats would be tabbies. Even so it is still exceedingly difficult to breed a pedigree tabby, whether long or shorthaired with the exacting pattern of markings required in the standard, which is the same for both. The longhair is even more difficult than the short, as even if the markings are good, it is not easy to distinguish a definite pattern in the long fur. Careful grooming will help to show it at its best, otherwise the pattern tends to fade into the background, appearing as smudges and patches.

Harrison Weir considered that tabbies were not among the original longhaired cats introduced into Europe from Persia but were the result of cross-matings with the resident shorthairs. The name 'tabby' is derived from Attibiya, a quarter in

Baghdad where watered silk was first made many centuries ago. The markings on the cats' coats resembled those on the material known as tabbisilk, so the cats were known as 'tabbies'. The dictionary gives 'tabby' as a kind of waved or watered silk and also as a female cat. This is really not correct as nowadays a tabby cat may be male or female.

The pattern of markings required for tabbies with classic markings is very complex. On the forehead the distinct marks should form a letter M, while around the eyes the delicate pencillings should be in the shape of a pair of spectacles. On the cheeks lines should form swirls following the contours. From above, the shoulder pattern should appear to be a large butterfly, made up of small ovals and two fairly wide bars running down the back on each side of the spine. Around the chest should run two unbroken lines, like necklaces, usually referred to as 'Lord Mayors' chains' after the splendid gold chains worn by Lord Mayors in Britain on ceremonial occasions. The tail should be evenly ringed, ending with a small solid tip. The legs, too, should be ringed, with the markings coming up to meet the body markings. The fur on the stomach should be the same as the all-over ground colouring but is frequently of a paler shade; it should bear small roundish solid markings. All the markings should stand out clearly from the background and there should be no brindling or blurring. No two cats are ever exactly alike in their markings and very few have the perfect pattern required.

Harrison Weir in his Points of Excellence—the standards he set for judging at the early shows—included brown, blue, silver, light grey, white, chocolate, mahogany, red and yellow, giving colour definitions for each. Interesting as these cats sound, the only colours recognized in Britain today are the red, brown and silver tabbies, while in North America blue and cream are also recognized. As well as the classic pattern of tabby markings, it is also possible to have tabbies with a pattern of markings known as mackerel, with the colours being the same as for those with the classic pattern. Such tabbies with long hair are rarely seen in Britain but mackerel markings do appear more frequently in the shorthaired tabbies.

The mackerel-tabby pattern differs considerably from the classic in that the markings should be as dense as possible and quite distinct from the ground colouring. The rings should be as narrow and numerous as possible and run vertically from the spine towards the ground. The tail must be neatly ringed and a chest ring or rings are most desirable.

## BROWN

These were very popular at the beginning of the century, being frequently Best in Show, but over the years the numbers have gradually decreased and, in Britain at least, they are now almost a rare pedigree variety. This is a great pity because they are much liked, particularly as pets, with the kittens always selling well. The difficulty has been, and still is, that with so few about, it is not always possible to find suitable males to keep the type and also to improve the pattern of markings.

Brown tabby mated to brown tabby could produce outstanding kittens but if carried on indefinitely may result in poor type. Different matings have been tried, including black, with the hope of intensifying the tabby markings, and blue to improve the type. Crossing with a silver tabby should be avoided as this may mean loss of eye colour. The standard for that variety calls for green or hazel eyes and these, once bred in, could prove exceedingly difficult to breed out. Brown tabbies may appear in litters where there is no history of such in the pedigree—for example from a blue mated to a red tabby and from a blue mated to a silver tabby.

Harrison Weir considered that tabby markings were first introduced into longhaired cats by matings with the English (British) tabby. However, he did write about a cat from Russia with long fur, 'the colour of a dark tabby, mostly of a dark brown'. It is quite probable that these Russian cats were used with other longhairs to produce some of the early brown tabbies.

This variety was a great favourite of Miss Frances Simpson. She thought they had 'more intelligent and expressive countenances than any other cats'. Her own brown tabby Persimmon was an outstanding cat in his day, siring some beautiful kittens. From his photograph he appears to have type quite comparable with modern cats and a full coat, although Miss Simpson does say in all honesty that the markings on his back were too heavy and he had a white under-lip, a fault found in many tabbies. She wrote also about King Humbert, another famous brown tabby of his time, who was exported to the

States in 1885 to Mr E. N. Barker, an American cat judge. King Humbert sired a number of excellent kittens, notably Jasper and Champion Crystal, both of which did very well at the shows. His owner refused $1,000 offered for him by a New York millionaire—a fantastic sum for a cat in those days.

At the early cat shows the class was often for brown tabby or sable cats and early fanciers suggested that the background colouring in the standard be given as sable. Sable tabbies would be a more appropriate name but the change has never been made.

When first born the kittens may be very dark, showing little of the future tabby markings and it may be many months before the pattern shows up distinctly. If choosing one for breeding, the kitten with the richest colouring would be the best choice.

Faults which appear are blurring of the markings, too solid markings on the back, white chins and tips to tail. The pattern of markings is as for the other tabbies.

## STANDARD

### BROWN

*Colour and Markings*—Rich tawny sable, with delicate black pencillings running down face. The cheeks crossed with two or three distinct swirls. The chest crossed by two unbroken narrow lines, butterfly markings on shoulders. Front of legs striped regularly from toes upwards. The saddle and sides to have deep bands running down, and the tail to be regularly ringed.

*Coat*—Long and flowing, tail short and full.

*Body*—Cobby and massive; short legs.

*Head*—Round and broad, small well-placed and well-tufted ears, short broad nose, full round cheeks.

*Eyes*—Large and round, hazel or copper colour.

### SCALE OF POINTS

| | |
|---|---:|
| Coat .... .... .... .... .... .... .... | 50 |
| Body .... .... .... .... .... .... .... | 15 |
| Head .... .... .... .... .... .... .... | 20 |
| Eyes .... .... .... .... .... .... .... | 15 |
| Total .... | 100 |

6 Two delightful Red Self kittens with very few markings

7 An attractive study of a Cream with good top to head

8  A Red Tabby showing tabby markings on the face

9  A proud **Silver** Tabby mother with her outstanding litter of four

SILVER

At the beginning of the century classes for the silver tabbies were well filled but, judging by early photographs and by the judges' reports of the show, they were not comparable with the modern silvers. Instead of long, pale-silver fur with the contrasting pattern of dense black markings, the ground coats were often blue, possibly due to cross-breeding and the markings were far from distinct, the backs often being solid black. The cat judges of that time said that the classes were often full of nondescript cats, neither tabby or silver.

Things did improve. The late Princess Victoria of Schleswig-Holstein, a noted cat breeder of her day, owned several and helped to make them fashionable. Mrs Slingsby's Champion Don Pedro of Thorpe and Lady Pink's Shrover II, among others, did much winning at the shows but gradually the numbers fell off.

Writing in 1930 in a revision of his book *Our Cats and All About Them*, published in 1912, Mr C. A. House, a cat judge and breeder, spoke 'with regret' of the silver tabbies as one of the varieties fallen 'from its former higher estate'. He put the blame on the fact that silver tabbies and chinchillas 'were more closely allied than they are today' and said that as the chinchilla breeders were in the majority in the society that was responsible for formulating the standards, it was agreed that the eye colour for both the chinchillas and the silver tabbies should be green. It is strange that there should have been this disagreement, as the silver tabbies were the older variety. Indeed it is always said that the chinchillas evolved in the first place from the silver tabbies, with both having hazel eyes in the early days.

It is exceedingly difficult to breed a silver tabby with the exacting markings required and one breeder advocates the occasional use of a shorthaired silver tabby to improve the pattern. Another suggests using a very good blue or black to improve the type, although this would possibly mean loss of eye colour. As brown tinges in the coats are faults, a brown tabby mating would certainly not improve the colour and may also result in brown tabbies appearing in litters from time to time.

The best kittens are darkest at birth, the markings only appearing as the fur grows—it may be several months before the true tabby pattern can be seen. In all the longhaired tabbies careful grooming is essential and it is quite an art to brush the fur so the markings stand out clearly.

Faults are brindling in the coat and yellow marks, particularly around the base of the tail.

## STANDARD

### SILVER

*Colour*—Ground colour pure pale silver, with decided jet-black markings; any brown tinge a drawback.

*Head*—Broad and round, with breadth between ears and wide at muzzle, short nose, small well-tufted ears.

*Shape*—Cobby body, short thick legs.

*Eyes*—Colour: Green or hazel.

*Coat and condition*—Silky in texture, long and dense, extra long on frill.

*Tail*—Short and bushy.

### SCALE OF POINTS

| | |
|---|---:|
| Colour .... .... .... .... .... .... | 40 |
| Head .... .... .... .... .... .... .... | 20 |
| Shape.... .... .... .... .... .... .... | 10 |
| Tail .... .... .... .... .... .... .... | 5 |
| Eyes (green or hazel) .... .... .... .... | 10 |
| Coat as condition .... .... .... .... .... | 15 |
| Total .... | 100 |

#### RED

There has been a great improvement in the type and colour of the red tabbies in recent years. Originally the background colour was more that of marmalade, not the rich mahogany red with the deeper red markings the standard called for. Red tabbies are very much liked, appearing to be a general favourite with men for some reason.

At the early shows they were known as oranges, and were shown in the same classes as the brown tabbies, but few had the markings required. Most had white chins and white tips to the tails, faults which still appear. It was not until the 1900s that there was any great improvement and this appears to have been brought about by the judicial use of black longhairs at studs. Pedigree red tabbies have always been few and far between and the two World Wars, with the almost complete cessation of breeding, meant that they almost vanished from the cat world scene. It was chiefly due to the late Mrs Campbell Fraser and Miss Lelgarde Fraser that the variety did survive and the Hendon red tabbies were once again appearing at the shows, winning many prizes.

Today there are a number of breeders interested in the variety, although those seen at the shows are comparatively few in number. It is because they are fairly rare that it is not always possible to mate red to red and in any case it is as well not to do so indefinitely as it has been found that the markings eventually become blurred and there may be some loss of type. Breeders advocate mating a tortoiseshell to a red tabby, which could produce red, tortoiseshell and black kittens, amongst others. Using a black to a red may also produce the same coloured kittens and in both cases some of the reds could be self, rather than tabby.

As the pattern of markings shows up clearly at birth, the most distinctive kitten then is the best one to keep for showing

## STANDARD

### RED

*Colour and markings*—Deep rich red colour, markings to be clearly and boldly defined, continuing down the chest, legs and tail.

*Coat*—Long, dense and silky; tail short and flowing, no white tip.

*Body*—Cobby and solid, short thick legs.

*Head*—Broad and round, small ears, well set and well tufted, short broad nose, full round cheeks.

*Eyes*—Large and round, deep copper colour.

### SCALE OF POINTS

| | | | | | | | |
|---|---|---|---|---|---|---|---|
| Coat .... | .... | .... | .... | .... | .... | .... | 50 |
| Body .... | .... | .... | .... | .... | .... | .... | 15 |
| Head .... | .... | .... | .... | .... | .... | .... | 20 |
| Eyes .... | .... | .... | .... | .... | .... | .... | 15 |
| | | | | | Total | .... | 100 |

or breeding. The markings may fade as the fur grows but by the age of five to six months the kitten should begin to live up to its early promise and show well-defined markings.

It is not easy to breed a cat with the correct pattern in a deep dark red standing out from the background colour of a rich red. The face markings are frequently good but the back may be too solid and lack the butterfly on the shoulders. The fur should be silky all over, not harsh along the spine as can occur.

Red tabbies are not all males. From pure red breeding, both male and female can be born but if from mixed parentage, the reds will be males and the females tortoiseshell or tortoiseshell and white. The red or sandy mongrel pet cats seen around, usually of unknown ancestry are, in most cases, male—which may account for the fallacy starting.

Faults are noses a little too long, upright ears, pale fur on the tummies and white hairs anywhere.

### BLUE

This variety is unknown in Britain but has been recognized in the United States since 1962. Harrison Weir mentioned blue tabbies in his original Points of Excellence but there is no similarity between the modern variety and them. They had bright-blue ground colouring with jet-black markings, while the American blue tabbies should have pale blueish fur with deeper-blue tabby markings and eyes of brilliant copper colour. It is a rare variety in America, seen infrequently at the shows.

### CREAM

Unknown in Britain, the cream tabby is recognized in America but is also comparatively rare there. The ground colour should be of palest cream, with buff or cream markings which should be of a darker hue than the background fur so that the tabby markings show up distinctly. The nose tip and paw pads should be pink and the big round eyes of brilliant copper.

The type is frequently good but it is very difficult to breed this variety to comply with the recognized standard, so that there is sufficient contrast between the background and the pattern of markings.

## Ticked, shaded and contrasting

### CHINCHILLAS

Known as one of the aristocrats of the Cat Fancy, the chinchillas are a most striking variety, with such adjectives as 'glamorous', 'ethereal' and 'fairy-like' being applied to them. They are also unusual for their pure white undercoats having delicate tippings of black, giving a shining silver effect and contrasting well with the emerald or blue-green eyes.

Although considered by some to be fairly new, chinchillas were in fact one of the first 'man-made' varieties. They are thought to have been evolved from silver tabbies and first appeared in the class 'silver tabbies, including blue tabbies, with or without white'. At the Crystal Palace show in 1894 they were given a class of their own for the first time. It is said that the first chinchillas were very lightly marked silver tabbies but in all probability they resulted from silver tabby crosses with blue—what would now be known as blue chinchillas. John Jennings in his book *Domestic or Fancy Cats*, published in 1893, wrote 'The Chinchilla is a peculiar but beautiful variety, the fur at the roots is silver, and shades to the tips to a decided slate hue, giving a most pleasing and attractive appearance.' Why the name 'chinchilla' was given is still a mystery but in the early catalogues, when they were shown in the mixed classes, the owners described their cats as 'silver chinchilla', 'chinchilla tabby' and so on, so this may be how the name arose.

A Mrs Vallence is credited with breeding one of the first chinchillas. According to Mr C. A. House, a judge and writer on cats in the early 1900s

> Chinnie was the result of a chance mating, a maiden of high degree being wooed by a gay and gallant roamer, who belonged to no one knew whom, and had no known home. Chinnie was of silver tone of colour but nothing approaching the colour of the chinchillas of today. It was really a light lavender.

Chinnie was mated to a male, Fluffy I, a pure silver with indefinite tabby markings and among the kittens they produced was one outstanding female called Beauty. Eventually this cat was mated to a light smoke Champion Perso and a male in her litter Silver Lambkin later became the first chinchilla stud. He may still be seen to this day, stuffed in the National History Museum at South Kensington, London, England. Any one, however, going to see him will be in for a disappointment. He looks very dark, short of coat, and bears no resemblance to the modern beauties of today.

Most chinchillas of that era were heavily ticked with bars and tabby markings and their eyes were more often than not golden brown in colour.

Some had light coats and some had dark and there appears to have been great confusion as to what really was required for the perfect chinchilla. In its wisdom, the Silver Society, founded in 1900, decided that there should be two varieties, the chinchilla with light tickings and the shaded silver with much heavier tickings and looking darker in appearance altogether. The standard set laid down that the chinchillas should be as pale and unmarked a silver as possible while the shaded silvers should have coats of pale, clear silver, shaded on the face, legs and backs but having as few tabby markings as possible. Both varieties could have eyes of green or orange. However, instead of making things easier, allowing two varieties appeared to have created even greater problems. Matters eventually came to a head when at one show a judge gave the same cat a special prize as a shaded silver and also one as a chinchilla. In 1902 the shaded silver standard was withdrawn, chinchillas only being recognized. This is still the case in Britain, but in America, Australia, New Zealand and other countries, the shaded silver is a recognized variety.

It soon became the aim to breed chinchillas with very light tickings; unfortunately this soon resulted in cats with lighter bones and some lacking stamina, faults which took some years to breed out.

Today's chinchillas are still inclined to be lighter boned than most other longhaired varieties but are by no means delicate. The black tippings on the pure white undercoat on the back, flanks, head, ears and tail give the chinchilla a sparkling appearance. Heavy ticking is considered a bad fault, as are any dark patches, bars, brown or yellow tinges in the coat. Careful grooming is necessary to make the fur stand up, thus displaying the coat at its best.

A striking feature is the gorgeous emerald or blue-green eye colour, emphasized by the black or brown rims to the eyes. The type should be as for other longhairs, the head being broad and round, the tufted ears small and well set. The body should be cobby on short thick legs; the tail short and bushy. The tip to the nose should be a brick red and the paw pads black or dark brown.

The kittens are very dark when first born, with bars and shadow rings on the tail. Although it is hard to imagine, when first seeing a tiny chinchilla kitten, that these markings will go, they rapidly fade as the kitten grows, and often the darkest

## STANDARD

### CHINCHILLA

*Colour*—The undercoat pure white, the coat on back, flanks, head, ears and tail being tipped with black; this tipping to be evenly distributed, thus giving the characteristic sparkling silver appearance: the legs may be very slightly shaded with the tipping, but the chin, ear tufts, stomach and chest must be pure white; any tabby markings or brown or cream tinge is a defect. The tip of the nose brick-red, and the visible skin on eyelids and the pads black or dark brown.

*Head*—Broad and round, with breadth between ears, which should be small and well tufted; wide at the muzzle; snub nose.

*Shape*—Cobby body; short thick legs.

*Eyes*—Large, round and most expressive; emerald or blue-green in colour.

*Coat and condition*—Silky and fine in texture, long and dense, extra long on frill.

*Tail*—Short and bushy.

### SCALE OF POINTS

| | |
|---|---|
| Colour | 25 |
| Head | 20 |
| Shape | 15 |
| Eyes | 15 |
| Coat and condition | 15 |
| Tail | 10 |
| Total | 100 |

marked of the litter becomes the adult with the most sparkling coat and eventually a champion.

### SHADED SILVER

Shaded silvers are popular in North America and many other countries but still have to be shown as Any Other Variety in Britain. The main difference between them and the chinchillas is the general appearance of the fur; the type and eye colouring required being identical. The shaded silver's coat should have far more tippings and shadings, particularly on the back, sides, face and tail. In the American standard, these are known collectively as 'the mantle', with the colour being like pewter rather than silver.

As it is possible for both varieties to appear in the same litter, it is not always possible for the breeder to know which is which for some time, particularly as the best chinchilla kittens may be very dark at birth.

### BLACK AND BLUE SMOKE

One of the most striking of all the longhaired varieties, the smoke may be mistaken at first glance for a black. It is not until the cat moves that the intriguing glimpses of the white under-colour is seen. Referred to frequently as 'the cat of contrasts', the smoke attracts much attention at the shows with its mask of dense black, silver frill and ear tufts, which contrast well with the deep copper eyes. The body colouring should be black, shading to silver on the sides; and the feet too should be black. The type should be as for other longhairs and nowadays is usually very good.

The smoke is one of the oldest varieties and is thought to have originated by the mixed breeding of blacks, whites and blues. At first being shown in the Any Other Variety class, by 1893 there were enough for them to be given a class on their own.

The first smoke champion was said to be Backwell Jogram owned by Mrs H. V. James. He sired a number of prize-winning kittens, many of which were exported to America. An early photograph shows him to have a very good mask and contrasts.

**10** An unusual picture of a Brown Tabby kitten, a very old but still rare pedigree variety

11 A charming Chinchilla, perfectly presented, showing the correct black rims to the eyes

12 A Shaded Silver not recognised in Britain but popular in other parts of the world

13 A Smoke, the cat of contrasts, showing silver ear tufts and frill

His ears look a little large compared with today's standards, but most of the early longhairs had this fault. It is only by looking at old photographs that one realizes how hard the fanciers have worked over the years and by selective breeding have gradually improved the type of most varieties until many of today's champions come very close to the set standard.

The dark shades were preferred in Britain but at first America liked them lighter, which worked out very well for the British fanciers, with the lighter coated cats, such as Watership Caesar being exported to the United States, there to win high honours, as did Cossy bred by Lady Marcus Beresford.

They are now a comparatively rare variety but on looking through old catalogues and stud books, it becomes apparent that they were once very popular. The stud book issued by the National Cat Club for the years 1900 to 1905 lists 16 males and 14 females, a quite incredible number. A winner of that time was Champion Peter of Castlethorpe who took first place at a number of shows. When he was exhibited at the Crystal Palace show in 1912, the judges' report said that he had a grand head, eyes and shape, with mask much improved in colour. There is no mention of his contrasts or colouring.

Good smokes are still difficult to breed. Smoke may be mated to smoke but eventually this could mean loss of type. Some breeders use a black male with good results. A silver tabby should never be used, as this may mean the introduction of stripes and other tabby markings which could be exceedingly difficult to breed out.

Grooming is all important, especially if a smoke is to be exhibited. The variety is one of the most difficult to present to perfection and some owners say that they are really at their best for only two months in the year. The coat responds so quickly to climate changes that every care must be taken to keep the cat out of the hot sun, which will give the fur a rusty tinge, while damp weather makes the coat inclined to cling and also gives it a brownish hue.

The kittens are born almost black and owners may not know for some weeks if they really will be black or smoke. Before now, they have been registered as blacks only to turn out to be outstanding smokes when early adults. Experienced breeders are usually able to tell the difference when the kittens are quite young, looking for and detecting minute little white marks in the fur as soon as they appear.

Like blacks, the kittens go through a rusty stage and it may be seven or eight months before the beautiful contrasting coat can be seen.

It is also possible to have blue smokes, with the distinctive colour contrast, but with blue replacing the black. While most attractive, the variety is not so striking as that of the black as the contrast is not so marked.

## STANDARD

### SMOKE

A smoke cat is a cat of contrasts, the undercolour being as ash-white as possible, with the tips shading to black, the dark points being most defined on the back, head and feet, and the light points on frill, flanks and ear-tufts.

*Colour*—Body: black, shading to silver on sides, flanks and mask. Feet: black, with no markings. Frill and ear-tufts: silver. Undercolour: as nearly white as possible.

*Coat*—Silky texture, long and dense, extra long frill.

*Head*—Broad and round, with width between the ears, which should be small and tufted; snub nose.

*Body*—Cobby, not coarse but massive; short legs.

*Eyes*—Orange or copper in colour, large and round in shape, pleasing expression.

*Tail*—Short and bushy.

### SCALE OF POINTS

| | |
|---|---:|
| Colour: Body, mask and feet, frill and ear-tufts and undercolour .... .... .... .... .... | 40 |
| Coat texture and condition.... .... .... .... | 10 |
| Head (including ears) .... .... .... .... | 20 |
| Body .... .... .... .... .... .... .... | 15 |
| Eyes .... .... .... .... .... .... .... | 10 |
| Tail .... .... .... .... .... .... .... | 5 |
| Total .... | 100 |

N.B.—The above is also the standard for blue smokes, except that where the word 'black' occurs, 'blue' should be substituted.

# Female only

## BLUE-CREAM

The blue-cream is a sex-linked variety, any males born invariably proving sterile. Cats with blue and cream coats were known as long ago as the end of the nineteenth century after the first creams, or fawns as they were called then, had appeared. The blue and cream 'oddities' were born in litters when various crossbreeding was tried but they were not thought to be of any importance. At first the coats were patched rather than intermingled and they were frequently called blue tortoiseshells.

It was gradually realized that not only were the creams improved by cross-mating with blues, but kittens with cream and blue coats were appearing regularly in the litters. (They are sometimes found in litters from tortoiseshells.) It was further realized that by mating a blue-cream to either a blue or a cream male, wonderfully varied litters could result. If mated to a blue, the kittens could be blue males, cream males, blue females and blue-creams, while if a cream was used it was possible to have male creams, female creams, blue males and blue-cream females. It was not until 1929 that recognition was given and soon cats with outstanding type were appearing at the shows.

The standard calls for the two colours to be softly intermingled, giving a shot-silk effect. There should be no solid patches, although a blaze, a stripe running from the forehead down to the nose, is liked.

In North America, a blue-cream should be patched, not intermingled, and the blue should predominate, with the solid cream patches being well defined. A solid paw, that is, a paw that is entirely blue or cream, is considered a fault in Britain but in America at least three paws should be solid cream.

Probably because of their mixed breeding, the kittens are usually very sturdy and full of life. No two blue-cream kittens are exactly alike in appearance and, as the litter may also contain blue kittens and cream kittens, they are an entrancing sight to see.

The type is usually very good but it is exceedingly difficult to breed a cat with no patching at all, to be faulted when being judged. A reddish tinge in the coat is also considered a fault, as is a predominance of one colour or the other.

Now is probably the heyday of the blue-cream in Britain, the classes at the shows being well filled, with many winning the highest awards.

## STANDARD

### BLUE-CREAM

*Colour and Markings*—To consist of blue and cream, softly inter-mingled; pastel shades.

*Coat*—To be dense and very soft and silky.

*Body*—Short, cobby and massive; short thick legs.

*Head*—Broad and round, tiny ears, well placed and well tufted short broad nose, colour intermingled on face.

*Eyes*—Deep copper or orange.

### SCALE OF POINTS

| | |
|---|---|
| Colour .... .... .... .... .... .... | 30 |
| Coat and condition .... .... .... .... .... | 20 |
| Body .... .... .... .... .... .... .... | 15 |
| Head .... .... .... .... .... .... .... | 20 |
| Eyes .... .... .... .... .... .... .... | 15 |
| | |
| Total .... | 100 |

#### TORTOISESHELLS

The tortoiseshells are considered by many to be the most fascinating of all cats with their patched coats of red, cream and black. A female-only variety, males have appeared from time to time but usually fail to sire. In the United States, one or two males are said to have fathered kittens but it is difficult to know whether or not they were true tortoiseshells with no tabby markings. As breeding has always been very much a question of luck, the variety has little ancestorial history. They did appear at the early cat shows but were mostly of unknown parentage.

The ideal tortoiseshell should have a coat of bright patches of red and cream, interspersed with black but many are rather sombre in appearance, with the black predominating. It is rather difficult to get the separate patches in the long fur as seen in the shorthaired variety. The paws too should have small patches and even the ears should be 'broken' too. A cream or red mark, a blaze, running down from the forehead to the nose is liked and certainly adds character to the face.

Breeding tortoiseshells is very much a hit or miss affair and many crosses are tried, including using black, cream or red self males but it is still a matter of luck if a kitten like the mother does appear in the litter. A black female bred from a tortie mother could be mated to a cream male and may produce blacks, tortoiseshells, blue-creams and reds among others. Use of a red tabby as a stud may mean the introduction of tabby markings which could prove exceedingly difficult to breed out.

The type is usually very good, as is the eye colouring. Faults are brindling (hairs of a different colouring appearing in the patches); white hairs; tabby markings, or too large patches of colour. The red in the coat should be bright and not a pale sandy shade.

Tortoiseshells make delightful pets, alert and lively, and usually prove excellent mousers and ratters should the occasion arise.

From time to time one hears of a male tortoiseshell that is said to be worth a fortune. The cat usually turns out to be a

## STANDARD

### TORTOISESHELL

*Colour*—Three colours, black, red and cream, well broken into patches; colours to be bright and rich and well broken on face.

*Coat*—Long and flowing, extra long on frill and brush.

*Body*—Cobby and massive; short legs.

*Head*—Round and broad; ears small, well-placed and well-tufted; short broad nose, full round cheeks.

*Eyes*—Large and round, deep orange or copper.

### SCALE OF POINTS

| | | | | | | | |
|---|---|---|---|---|---|---|---|
| Coat .... | .... | .... | .... | .... | .... | .... | 50 |
| Body .... | .... | .... | .... | .... | .... | .... | 15 |
| Head .... | .... | .... | .... | .... | .... | .... | 20 |
| Eyes .... | .... | .... | .... | .... | .... | .... | 15 |

| | | |
|---|---|---|
| | Total .... | 100 |

hard-to-sex female, or to have tabby markings, and even if a male, would certainly not be worth a lot of money, as in all probability he proves to be sterile, with no value except as a curio.

### TORTOISESHELL AND WHITE (*Calico*)

This is another most striking female-only variety, closely allied to the tortoiseshell, with red, cream and black patching but having the addition of white. Once known as the chintz cat in Britain and still as the calico in North America, they are a much liked variety but are also comparatively rare. They are sometimes found on farms, having resulted from the mixed breeding of various coloured cats but these ones are usually short-coated.

As there were no males, the practice in the past was to use one of the self-coloured studs, not always successfully. The litters resulting were certainly attractive, of mixed colours, but rarely containing tortoiseshells and whites. More recently, thanks to the efforts of one breeder in Britain, more tortoiseshells and whites are appearing. By mating bicolour studs bred

## STANDARD

## TORTOISESHELL AND WHITE

*Colour*—Three colours, black, red and cream, to be well distributed and broken and interspersed with white.

*Coat*—Long and flowing, extra long on brush and frill.

*Body*—Cobby and massive; short legs.

*Head*—Round and broad; ears small, well-placed and tufted; short broad nose, full round cheeks.

*Eyes*—Large and round, deep orange or copper.

### SCALE OF POINTS

| | | | | | | | |
|---|---|---|---|---|---|---|---|
| Coat .... | .... | .... | .... | .... | .... | .... | 50 |
| Body .... | .... | .... | .... | .... | .... | .... | 15 |
| Head .... | .... | .... | .... | .... | .... | .... | 20 |
| Eyes .... | .... | .... | .... | .... | .... | .... | 15 |

|  |  |  |
|---|---|---|
| Total | .... | 100 |

from tortie and white mothers to tortie and whites, Miss N. Woodifield has successfully bred kittens like the mothers. She advocates using either a red and white or black and white bicolour male as sire but whatever stud is used, the kittens will certainly be most distinctive and highly intelligent.

The type is usually very good. Faults are too much white, although too little is just as bad and a white blaze on the forehead is much liked. The patches must be quite distinct, with no intermingling of the colour, or white hairs in the coloured patching, and there must be no tabby markings.

One often hears the same story with these cats too that a male is worth a small fortune. It is quite untrue. Any males born are invariable sterile.

The tortoiseshell and whites are strong healthy cats and make excellent mothers. A short daily grooming seems to keep them looking immaculate, with the fur rarely matting up as it does with some of the other longhaired varieties.

## Unusual varieties

### COLOUR-POINTS OR HIMALAYANS

Comparatively speaking, this is a modern, man-made variety but over the years many fanciers have toyed with the idea of producing a cat with the coat pattern of a Siamese: a pale body colouring with contrasting points with the full flowing fur of a longhair.

As far back as 1922, in Sweden, a Dr K. Tjebbes tried crossing Siamese with longhaired whites but apparently nothing further came of this. In 1924 in the United States cats with similar colouring were bred and were known as Malayan Persians but again they faded into obscurity. A few years after this, also in the United States, Dr Clyde Keeler and Mrs Virginia Cobb produced longhaired Siamese by crossing longhairs and Siamese but these did not prove very popular. Mrs Cobb went on to try further crosses but World War II saw the end of this breeding programme.

In 1935 in England a Mrs Barton-Wright started an Experimental Breeders Club with the object of breeding cats on much the same lines as Mrs Cobb and a kitten bred by her, from a mating of a Siamese with a blue longhair, went to Miss D. Collins, who registered her as Kala Dawn.

Shortly after the end of the war, one of Dawn's kittens, Kala Sabu, was sold to Mr Brian Stirling-Webb to use in his planned breeding of colour-points. He had become interested in the possibilities of producing such a pedigree variety, after a stray with surprisingly good type and Siamese coat pattern had been brought to him to be mated to his Siamese stud. With his profound knowledge of genetics he was able to work out a scientific breeding programme. He knew that it was possible to breed a Siamese with long fur in only two generations but to produce a cat with the true longhair type would take much longer. By using outstanding blues and blacks and crossing them with the first colour-points, he succeeded in greatly improving the type and, eventually, in 1955 they were granted recognition by the Governing Council of the Cat Fancy. Mr Stirling-Webb was still endeavouring to improve the variety at his death but Mrs S. Harding, who had been working closely with him for many years, carried on on the same lines successfully producing outstanding colour-points, bearing the Mingchiu prefix, which are now exported all over the world.

By a strange coincidence, in the United States, without realizing it but at the same time as Mr Stirling-Webb, Mrs M. Goforth was endeavouring to produce similar cats, which she called Himalayan after the rabbits and mice with similar colouring. Recognition was given in 1957.

In Canada, Mr and Mrs B. Borrett, of Chestermere fame, were also breeding Himalayans. They visited Mr B. Stirling-Webb's cattery and imported several of his Briarry cats to cross-breed with the home-bred Himalayans.

The general standard for the colour-points is the same for all colours, with the fur to be long and thick, the heads broad and round, the noses short with distinct stops and the ears small and tufted. The type should in no way resemble the Siamese. The eyes should be large, round and decidely blue in colour.

It is possible to breed colour-points with a variety of points colourings: seal, with cream body colour; blue, with glacial-white body colour; chocolate with ivory body colour; lilac, with magnolia; red with off-white; tortie with cream body colour. A blaze is liked in the tortie-points, which is invariably a female-only variety. Rarely a male is born, but he is usually sterile. Cream and other colours are also possible.

While breeding the early colour-points, both Mr Stirling-

14 An adorable Cream kitten with Blue Cream litter sister showing her well intermingled coat

15 A Tortoiseshell and White, with good patched coat, very intrigued with the guinea pig

16 A Tortoiseshell bred in France, showing blaze on face which is much liked

17 A Colourpoint with outstanding type and very good Seal points

Webb and Mrs S. Harding realized that it was possible to produce self chocolate and self lilac also. Mrs S. Harding has now produced some attractive cats but these varieties have not yet been recognized.

When first born the colour-points are white or cream in colour, with pink noses and foot pads and ears. In a few days

## STANDARD

### COLOUR-POINT

*Coat*—Fur long, thick and soft in texture, frill full.

    Colour (i) Seal points with cream body colour.
          (ii) Blue points with glacial-white body colour.
         (iii) Chocolate points with ivory body colour.
        (iv) Lilac points with magnolia body colour.
         (v) Red points with off-white body colour.
        (vi) Tortie points with cream body colour.

    Colours i–v inclusive—Points to be of solid colour and body shading, if any, to tone with the points.
    Colour vi—Points colour of tortie-points to be restricted to the basic seal colour, body shading, if any, to tone with points.

*Head*—Broad and round with width between the ears. Short face and short nose with distinct break or stop. Ears small and tufted and cheeks well developed.

*Eyes*—Large, round and full. Clear, bright and decidely blue.

*Body*—Cobby and low on leg.

*Tail*—Short and full, not tapering. A kink shall be considered a defect.

N.B.—Any similarity in *type* to Siamese, in particular a long straight nose to be considered most undesirable and incorrect.

### SCALE OF POINTS

| | |
|---|---|
| Coat .... .... .... .... .... .... .... | 15 |
| Points and body colour .... .... .... .... | 10 |
| Head .... .... .... .... .... .... .... | 30 |
| Shape of eye .... .... .... .... .... .... | 10 |
| Colour of eye.... .... .... .... .... .... | 10 |
| Body .... .... .... .... .... .... .... | 15 |
| Tail .... .... .... .... .... .... .... | 10 |
| Total .... | 100 |

D

the points colouring starts to appear, though at first it may be a little difficult to know what the ultimate colouring will be.

Affectionate, friendly, with quiet voices, the colour-points make delightful and distinctive pets. The numbers seen at the shows are increasing all the time, with the classes being well-filled.

BIRMANS

An unusual longhaired variety with the coat pattern of the Siamese, that is, having light body colouring with contrasting points, the Birman has the added and distinctive feature of four white-gloved paws. Known in France for over 30 years, one theory is that the Birmans arose in the first place by cross-matings of Siamese and longhairs but legend has it that they are a very old variety which originated in Burma, hence they are also known as the sacred cats of Burma.

It is said that centuries ago white cats were the guardians of the temple of Lao-Tsun and the much revered companions of the Kittah priests there. When the temple was attacked by raiders, the most venerable of all the priests, Mun-Ha, knelt in front of Tsun-Kyan-Kse, the golden goddess, with sapphire eyes and, with his beautiful white cat Sinh by his side, prayed for deliverance. Whilst praying, he died and Sinh, facing the goddess, placed his paws on his master's body. As he did this, his white fur took on the golden hue of the light reflected from the goddess, his eyes became the same deep blue as hers and his face, ears, feet and tail took on the colour of mother earth but where his paws touched his master, they remained white, a symbol of purity. The other priests stood amazed at this miracle and, as Sinh turned and stared at them, they were inspired and turned and attacked the raiders, sending them fleeing from the temple. Sinh stayed by the body for seven days without food or water and then he died, carrying his master's soul to Paradise. As the priests met to choose a new leader from among them, the hundred temple cats came into the chamber. No longer white, their colouring had become the same as Sinh and their eyes as deep a blue. Quietly they formed a circle round the youngest priest, Ligoa, and so the new High Priest was chosen.

Centuries later, in 1916, rebellion again threatened the safety of the priests and the cats but, thanks to help given by a Major Gordon Russell and Monsieur Auguste Pavie, disaster was averted. Major Russell went to live in France and in 1919 a pair of the sacred cats was sent to him as a token of the priests' gratitude. Unfortunately the male died on the voyage but the female and the litter she was expecting lived and so for a while the breed was established in France, being recognized in 1925. The Second World War meant practically the end of cat breeding there but a pair of Birmans survived to re-establish the variety eventually. Thanks to the efforts of breeders such as Madame Poirier, Madame Moulin and Madame Drossier, to mention a few, by the middle of the 1960s Birmans were appearing at the shows once again.

Up to then they were unknown in Britain but in 1964–5, Mrs E. Fisher and Mrs M. Richards imported the first seen there. They appeared at the shows in the Any Other Colour classes but by 1966 had been recognized and granted championship status. Among the first champions in Britain were Champion Paranjoti Chimea and Champion Paranjoti Katmandu and Birmans have since been exported to many countries throughout the world.

In 1960 a pair of Tibetan temple kittens was sent to Mrs G. Griswold in the United States. These were a thank-you present from a Mr Carter Townes who had recently been on holiday in the States and, while there, his cats Schiaffa and Boke Khmer had been looked after by Mrs Griswold. The kittens were his cats' progeny and the coat and points' colouring were the same as that of the Birmans. Investigations as to their origin revealed that the history was identical to that of the sacred cats of Burma, even down to the hundred cats. It is believed that some Kittah priests had fled into Cambodia when the fighting was on, taking their precious cats with them. The slight difference was that the Tibetan cats, more often than not, had only a few white toes instead of completely white paws.

A cat fancier in the United States was struck by the close resemblance to the Tibetan temple cats by the sacred cats of Burma then being bred in France. Soon Mrs Griswold and Madame Poirier, the well-known French breeder, were in correspondence, and eventually exchanged kittens. Mrs Griswold exhibited and won at the shows in Europe where the

Birmans were recognized but in the United States they were only seen in the experimental classes until they were recognized in 1967. Miss V. Clum, another well-known American breeder, had also become interested in Birmans and before long her cats, Opom De Lao Tsun of Gaylands and International Champion Neko De Lao Tsun of Gaylands were doing well at the shows.

Said to have enchanting personalities, these cats are becoming very popular and in Britain new importations both from France and Germany are helping to keep up the high standard. They are now being bred with point colourings of seal, blue, chocolate and lilac.

The Birmans differ from most longhairs in being comparatively long in the body, rather than cobby and with tails longish and bushy. The noses too are not so snub.

## STANDARD

### BIRMAN

*Body*—Long but low on the legs. Short strong paws. Four white paws, the white on the rear paws to go up the back of the legs to a point like a gauntlet.

*Head*—Wide, round but strongly built, with full cheeks.

*Fur*—Long with good full ruff, bushy tail, silky texture, slightly curled on belly.

*Eyes*—Bright China blue.

*Tail*—Bushy (not short).

*Colour and condition*—The colouring is the same as Siamese, seal and blue but face (mask) tail and paws are dark brown, in the seals and blue/grey in the blues. However, the beige of the coat is slightly golden. The paws are white gloved, this being the characteristic of the Birman cat.

### SCALE OF POINTS

| | | |
|---|---|---:|
| Body | .... .... .... .... .... .... | 20 |
| Head | .... .... .... .... .... .... | 20 |
| Fur | .... .... .... .... .... .... | 25 |
| Eyes | .... .... .... .... .... .... | 5 |
| Tail | .... .... .... .... .... .... | 10 |
| Colour and condition | .... .... .... .... | 20 |
| | Total .... | 100 |

BICOLOURS

The writers on early cats referred to cats with two-coloured coats and a number appeared at the early shows. Harrison Weir in his Points of Excellence gave a whole list of the possible colours with white for such cats. These, however, were short-haired and no standards were given for the longhairs, so obviously they were few in number. They were exhibited in the Any Other Colour class and could be blue and white, orange and white, tabby and white and black and white—the latter being most liked.

The black and whites, referred to as magpies, had dense black coats, with white feet, chests and noses and white blazes running up the centre of the face and were most attractive. The United States also had the two-coloured cats and, at the early shows, the orange and white and the blue and white were given their own classification.

Over the years, the bicoloured cats continued to be shown in the Any Other Colour class in Britain but, although much liked, little interest was shown in them from a breeding point of view and the kittens were usually sold as pets and neutered. It was not until a noted breeder, Miss N. Woodifield of Pathfinder fame, realized that by working on certain lines, bicolours could be used to produce the most elusive tortoiseshell and whites. In 1966 the bicolours were granted recognition but, unfortunately, the approved standard was found to be impossible to reproduce to order. It was based on the markings required for a Dutch rabbit and required such definite colour divisions that cats with such coat colourings were seldom, if ever, born, with the result that challenge certificates were mostly withheld by the judges. Breeders became discouraged as it was almost impossible to make a cat a champion. Eventually, in 1971, the standard was amended and the coat was required to be not more than two-thirds coloured and not more than half to be white. Any colour with white is allowed. The United States' standards are similar. There are now a number of champions, many bearing the Pathfinder prefix and several have been exported to the United States, where they are recognized by the Cat Fanciers' Association.

Bicolours may be mated to bicolours but to improve the type it may be necessary from time to time to use a self-coloured male but this may result in self-coloured kittens in future generations. By careful cross-breeding, tortoiseshells and tortoiseshells and whites may result.

Bicolours should have the same type as for most other longhairs: broad heads, short noses, neat ears and big orange or copper eyes. The full luxurious coats should show definite divisions of colour with the white and there should be no white hairs mixed in with the colours.

The mixed breeding that was necessary to produce the variety has resulted in strong healthy cats, the males being quite large. Crossing the colours may result in kittens with tricoloured coats which are most striking and much liked as pets.

## STANDARD

### BICOLOUR

*Colours and distribution*—Any solid colour and white, the patches of colour to be clear, even and well distributed. Not more than two thirds of the cats coat to be coloured and not more than a half to be white. Face to be patched with colour and white.

*Coat*—Silky texture. Long and flowing, extra long on frill and tail.

*Head*—Round and broad with width between the ears which should be small, well placed and tufted. Short broad nose, full cheeks, wide muzzle and firm chin (level bite).

*Body and legs*—Body cobby and massive, short thick legs.

*Eyes*—Large and round, set well apart, deep orange or copper in colour.

*Tail*—Short and full.

*Serious faults*—Tabby markings. A long tail. Yellow or green eyes.

### SCALE OF POINTS

| | | | | | | | |
|---|---|---|---|---|---|---|---:|
| Colour | .... | .... | .... | .... | .... | .... | 25 |
| Coat .... | .... | .... | .... | .... | .... | .... | 15 |
| Body .... | .... | .... | .... | .... | .... | .... | 15 |
| Tail .... | .... | .... | .... | .... | .... | .... | 5 |
| Head .... | .... | .... | .... | .... | .... | .... | 25 |
| Eyes .... | .... | .... | .... | .... | .... | .... | 15 |
| | | | | | Total | .... | 100 |

TURKISH

Turkish cats are in all probability one of the oldest varieties of long-coated cats known, differing only from the original pure white angoras in having auburn markings as well.

They were introduced into England about 1956 by Miss L. Lushington and Miss S. Halliday who, whilst travelling in the area around the great Van lake in Turkey, were struck by the very distinctive appearance of several cats they saw, wondering what kind they were. They noticed too that they would swim of their own accord in shallow rivers and pools in the hot weather, unlike most other cats they knew that would not go into water unless they had to. After making many enquiries, they managed to find an unrelated breeding pair, which eventually were imported into England. They proved to breed true and further pairs were imported. It is not easy to find these cats nor is it easy to get permission to bring them out of Turkey. They are obviously descendants of the old variety but it was impossible to trace the pedigrees as until recently the Turkish people had failed to realize that there would be so much interest in them and no records had been kept.

Angoras are now being bred at the Ankara Zoo but these are white only. Several pairs have been imported into the United States, where a planned breeding programme is being carried on. They are referred to as the Turkish angoras and have their own standard, with a number of fanciers now producing them. As yet there are no Turkish cats, as recognized in Britain— white with auburn markings—in the United States.

In spite of the fact that it was realized that the Turkish cats introduced into England did breed true, in that the characteristics of the kittens were the same as those of the parents, recognition could not be granted immediately. To obtain recognition by the Governing Council of the Cat Fancy in Britain, it is necessary to be able to produce a pedigree showing four generations of pure breeding and also to show that a number of breeders are interested in a certain variety. As there were so few Turkish cats about, owing to the difficulties of finding suitable pairs and to the time and cost of quarantine, it was not until 1969, 13 years since the first one was seen in England, that the standard was approved and championship status granted.

The first Turkish cats were exhibited as Any Other Colour and they bore such names as Atalya Anatolia and Burdor. Miss Lushington registered her prefix as Van and soon cats and kittens with this prefix were appearing at the shows. There are now a number of other breeders of this variety bearing such prefixes as Vandaha, Cayeli and Moroni—to mention one or two.

Seen side by side there would be no question of confusing Turkish with Persian cats, as the type is quite different. Whereas the heads of the latter are broad and round, with small ears and short noses, those of the Turkish are wedge-shaped, the

## STANDARD

### TURKISH

*Colour and coat*—Chalk white with no trace of yellow. Auburn markings on face with white blaze. Ears white; nose tip, pads and inside ears a delicate shell pink. Fur long, soft and silky to the roots; woolly undercoat.

*Head*—Short wedge; well-feathered large ears, upright and set fairly close together; long nose.

*Eyes*—Round, colour light amber, rims pink-skinned.

*Body*—Long but sturdy, legs medium in length; neat round feet with well-tufted toes. Males should be particularly muscular on neck and shoulders.

*Tail*—Full, medium length, auburn in colour with faint auburn rings in cats, more distinct ring markings in kittens.

### SCALE OF POINTS

| | |
|---|---|
| Colour and coat .... .... .... .... .... | 35 |
| Head .... .... .... .... .... .... .... | 25 |
| Eyes .... .... .... .... .... .... .... | 10 |
| Body .... .... .... .... .... .... .... | 10 |
| Brush .... .... .... .... .... .... .... | 10 |
| Condition .... .... .... .... .... .... | 10 |
| Total .... | 100 |

Note: this is the ideal; some cats may have small auburn markings irregularly placed but this should not disqualify an otherwise good specimen.

18 A Birman showing the distinctive white gloved paws

19 A demure Bi-Colour with clear division between the two colours, as required in the standard

20 A Cameo produced in Britain by selective breeding, but not yet an official variety there

21 A Self Chocolate, an excellent example of a man-made variety

22 Turkish cat with chalk white coat and showing the correct auburn markings and ringed tail

ears large and upright and the noses longish. The noses are pink tipped and the eyes amber.

The chalk-white fur is long and silky but without the fluffy appearance of most long-coated cats, as it lacks the woolly undercoat. Because of the extreme climate in the Van area from which they originated, the Turkish seem to lose most of their coats in the summer—and may look almost short-coated— they grow them again very quickly as the weather gets colder.

Having no undercoat, they are one of the easiest longhaired varieties to groom, as long as this is done daily. A light combing only is advised as too liberal use of a brush is inclined to make the fur springy. The distinctive auburn markings should be on the face only but some do have small patches of colouring on the body as well. The tails should be ringed with alternate light and dark auburn.

Compared with the female, the male has a most definite muscular appearance, with powerful neck and shoulders.

The litters average four and even when the kittens are newly born, the auburn markings show up most clearly on the white fur. They develop quickly, being more forward than some other long-coated varieties and appear to be able to climb and play when only a few weeks old. The Turkish are very affectionate and certainly most lovable and, if not used for breeding, make delightful neutered pets.

ANY OTHER COLOUR OR VARIETY

At the early cat shows in Britain there were classes for the white, black and tabby longhairs but all other colours could only be shown in the class known as 'Any Other Colour or Variety'. As few colours had recognized standards in those days, this enabled any variation to be exhibited. Most varieties, such as the blues, first appeared in these classes, which to begin with were very large but, as more varieties received recognition, the entries grew fewer and fewer. At one time, it appeared as if the class would have to be dropped as so few cats were being shown in it.

In the list of varieties recognized by the British Governing Council is 13a 'Any Other Colour', which may seem strange, as it is not possible to have a set standard for this, but as all cats must be registered before they may be exhibited, this enables those entered under this heading to be exhibited in classes specially put on for them. They do not compete with the fully recognized varieties and cannot become champions.

Into this classification go cats which have resulted from mis-mating, cross-breeding, or are a new variety making its debut to the public after years of carefully planned breeding, as the colour-points (Himalayans) did. A cat registered under this heading may have a pedigree but does not conform to the requirements necessary for any specific recognized variety. Three generations of pure breeding are required before consideration can be given by the GCCF for a request for a breed number and an agreed standard. There must also be enough breeders interested in producing them. Once a variety does receive recognition, a cat may be re-registered as such and can then compete in the Open Breed class, possibly eventually becoming a champion, if this status has been granted.

Almost anyone can breed a cat that looks different in some way or another from the already-known pedigree varieties but it is not an easy matter to reproduce such a variation to order, unless simple genetics are understood. It is an expensive business to produce a new variety and may take some years, probably involving a number of experimental matings, and the consequent neutering and finding of homes for kittens that are not exactly what is required.

In Britain, at the moment, the classes are quite large and may include such new varieties in the making as self-lilac and self-chocolate longhairs, both of which it is hoped will receive recognition in the near future. The chocolate should have rich chestnut-coloured fur and the lilac, being a dilute form of the brown, a pale, brownish lilac rather than a pale blue. The type should be as for other longhairs.

Cameos are also appearing in this class (see Cameos) as are blue chinchillas resulting from the cross-matings of blue Persians and chinchillas. The type is usually very good, but the sea-green eye colouring is lost and blue replaces the white in the coat.

MAINE COON

Maine coon cats have been known in the United States for more than a hundred years. They are thought to have originated in the first place from the interbreeding of the resident shorthaired cats in Maine with longhairs taken there by sailors and other travellers. Massive, hardy cats, the name given them arose in the first place from the resemblance of their fur to that of the racoon. They were said to have resulted from cat/racoon matings, now known to be biologically quite impossible. For many years they have had their own show in Maine when the Maine State Champion Cat of the Year is chosen.

Larger in size than most cats, their silky flowing fur is not quite so long as that of most longhairs but having no undercoat is very easy to groom. Their heads are medium in size, with longish noses and the ears are large and tufted. The big round eyes may be green or a colour in keeping with the coat, which may be any colour or colours. The muscular body stands on sturdy tall legs and the long full tail should taper at the end.

They may now compete for championships at most shows and the kittens are much in demand. They are not known in Britain, although some domestic pets look very similar.

CAMEOS

First produced in 1954 in the United States by Dr Rachel Salisbury, they were developed in the first instance from smoke and tortoiseshell matings. Silvers and reds have also been used in their development. Chinchilla crosses were also used but the introduction of the beautiful emerald or sea-green eye colouring had proved difficult to breed out.

Cameos are now being bred in Australia, New Zealand and in Europe. In Britain a few fanciers have been very interested in breeding cameos, several most successfully, but the numbers have not increased significantly during the last few years and cameos have not yet received recognition.

It is possible for a cameo to be red- or cream-tipped but at present the United States' standards state that the colour should be red. A number of variations are possible.

In the shell cameo, the undercoat should be ivory white, with delicate red ticking on the back, flanks, head and tail. The face and legs may be slightly shaded with tickings but the chin, ear tufts, stomach and chest should be white without ticking. There should be no signs of tabby markings or bars. The eyes may be copper or gold and the rims to the eyes and the tip to the nose should be rose coloured. It is also possible to have a shaded cameo with fur of pure red with no markings but with a definite gradual shading down the sides to blend in with the pale-ivory ground colour on the underside.

Another attractive variation is the smoke cameo, known also as the red smoke, with deep, reddish-beige fur and ivory to light-cream undercoat. The contrasting face mask, paws and tail should be a rich red, with the frill and ear tufts whitish and the eyes copper or gold. Also recognized is the tabby cameo, with ground colouring of pale cream broken with well-defined red or beige markings. It is also possible to have a cameo tortoiseshell, with silvery-white undercoat and tortoise-shell tickings.

Cameos may be born looking almost white and, as the fur grows, the definite colouring begins to show, the shaded looking darker than the shell and the smokes even darker.

### PEKE-FACED

The Peke-faced is not a separate variety but, while the characteristics required are the same for most other longhairs, the Peke-faced has a head very much like that of the Pekinese dog. The nose should be very short with a marked stop and indentation between the eyes; the broad muzzle should be decidedly wrinkled and the eyes should be large and round, set wide apart.

The Peke-faced is recognized in two colours: the red self, that is, without markings, and the red tabby, with pattern of markings as for other tabbies. They appear in litters of red self and red tabbies and, while once popular in the United States, now appear at the shows in smaller numbers.

They are unrecognised in Britain, as it is considered that the short noses and deep nose breaks may produce breathing problems and jaw malformations.

### BALINESE

Unknown in Britain, the Balinese appeared first in the early 1950s in the United States in litters from pure-bred Siamese. Siamese in type, these kittens had fluffy, silky coats and at first were looked on as 'throw-outs', being either neutered and sold as pets, or destroyed. Most unexpectedly, they kept on appearing and one or two breeders became interested in these longhaired Siamese. Eventually it was discovered that when mated together they would breed true—the litters were entirely like the parents in looks.

There was some confusion at first as it was thought that they were similar to the colour-points, known as Himalayans in North America. The only similarity between these two varieties is in the colourings, both having the Siamese coat pattern: light body colouring with contrasting points. The colour-points are entirely longhair in type, whereas the Balinese are Siamese in type and personality.

The Balinese is a lithe dainty cat, with medium-sized, wedge-shaped head, large pointed ears and almond-shaped eyes of deep vivid blue. The svelte body stands on long slender legs and the long tail tapers to a point. The fine and silky fur is not as long as that of most other longhairs, being about two inches or more in length. They are now being bred in a number of Siamese points' colourings, such as seal, chocolate, blue and lilac and have been granted full championship status by all the North American registering bodies.

CYMRIC

The Cymric is unknown in Britain. It has typical Manx type but a full long coat instead of the usual short fur of the normal Manx. The Cymric has been bred in the United States from the longhaired, tailless kittens that appeared from time to time in Manx litters. They have now been developed as a separate variety but have not yet received championship status.

The characteristics are the same as for the recognized Manx: the head is large and round with full cheeks, the nose is slightly long and the eyes are large and round; the body is short and the hindquarters are high, giving the typical rabbit-like gait when walking; the rump should be round, with a hollow where the tail should start but this is not so easily seen in the long fur. All colours and coat patterns have been produced. As they are so unusual, they have attracted a great deal of interest in the United States, where they have been given the name Cymric, although there appears to be no known connection with Wales.

### A NOTE ON NORTH AMERICA

The types of longhair found almost exclusively in North America have already been mentioned. But, although cats and cat lovers have much in common the world over, there are a few differences as regards standards that ought to be mentioned. In the United States the majority of cats with long hair come under the heading 'Persians', with the general standard being the same for all colours, as follows: white, blue-eyed, copper-eyed, and odd-eyed, black, blue, red, cream, chinchilla, shaded silver, red chinchilla (shell cameo), red shaded (shaded cameo), black smoke, blue smoke and red smoke (cameo smoke). There are also the tabbies (classic or mackerel tabby pattern) in silver, red, brown, blue, cream and cameo varieties in this category. Finally, there are the tortoiseshell, calico (tortoiseshell and white), blue-cream, Peke-face red and Peke-face red tabby and the bicolour. The white, black, blue, red and creams are referred to as solid colours, rather than self as in Britain for example.

Separate status is given to the angora, Balinese, Birman (sacred cat of Burma), Himalayan (colour-point) and Maine coon.

There are nine registering bodies and each has its own standards but the overall picture is much the same, only the wording differing slightly. The following is the standard for Persians as recognized by the Cat Fanciers' Association Inc.:

## STANDARD

### PERSIANS

*Head*—Round and massive, with great breadth of skull; round face with round underlying bone structure; well set on a short, thick neck.

*Nose*—Short, snub and broad, with break.

*Cheeks*—Full.

*Jaws*—Broad and powerful.

*Chin*—Full and well developed.

*Ears*—Small, round-tipped, tilted forward, and not unduly open at the base; set far apart, and low on the head, fitting into (without distorting) the rounded contour of the head.

*Eyes*—Large, round and full; set far apart and brilliant, giving a sweet expression to the face.

*Body*—Of cobby type, low on the legs, deep in the chest, equally massive across the shoulders and rump, with a short, well-rounded middle piece; large or medium in size; quality the determining consideration, rather than size.

*Back*—Level.

*Legs*—Short, thick and strong; forelegs straight.

*Paws*—Large, round and firm; toes carried close, five in front and four behind.

*Tail*—Short but in proportion to body length; carried without a curve and at an angle lower than the back.

*Coat*—Long and thick, standing off from the body; of fine texture, glossy and full of life; long all over the body, including the shoulders; the ruff immense and continuing in a deep frill between the front legs; ear and toe tufts long; brush very full.

Withhold awards: locket or button; kinked or abnormal tail; incorrect number of toes.

(With acknowledgement to the Cat Fancier's Association Inc.)

## SCALE OF POINTS

| | |
|---|---|
| Head (including size and shape of eyes, ear shape and set) .... .... .... .... .... .... | 30 |
| Type (including shape, size, bone and length of tail) | 20 |
| Coat .... .... .... .... .... .... .... | 10 |
| Condition .... .... .... .... .... .... | 10 |
| Colour .... .... .... .... .... .... | 20 |
| Eye colour .... .... .... .... .... .... | 10 |
| Total .... | 100 |

In all tabby varieties, the 20 points for colour are to be divided between markings and colour, with 10 for colour.

The standards for the Birmans and Himalayans (colour-points) are very similar to those in Britain, as is that for the angora to the Turkish but they are set out in far more detail.

The Canadian standards are similar to the American ones, with a wealth of detail.

From a judging point of view generally, the Persians in North America are slightly more strongly to type than those seen in Britain, that is, they have shorter, flatter noses.

Chapter three

# Pet cats and pet care

## Choosing a kitten

Careful thought is needed before deciding to buy a kitten. In the excitement at the idea of owning a beautiful longhair for the first time, the disadvantages may be overlooked but they should be taken into consideration before a definite decision is reached.

Whatever variety is chosen, it should be remembered that, barring accidents, most cats live a long life, with nowadays even 20 or 25 not being unknown. As the owner you will be responsible for the feeding, daily grooming and general welfare of the cat. That means giving affection, attention and companionship as well. Furthermore arrangements will have to be made during the holidays for the cat to be put in a boarding cattery or looked after by friends, either at your home or in their house.

On the other hand you will be buying a decorative pet that will soon grow up to be a most distinctive-looking cat and one that will be a charming companion for many years to come.

Having read about the various varieties—but apart from that knowing little about them—before making a final choice, it is as well to visit a cat show and see the variety that appeals to you the most. It will also be possible there to meet the breeders and probably arrange to visit the house and see the conditions under which the kittens have been bred.

Once having settled on a particular variety, you must decide on either a male or female. If buying purely as a pet, with no intention of breeding, the kitten should be neutered as soon as old enough, so it does not matter a great deal which sex is

E

chosen. Neutering, or spaying, a female is a more serious operation than that of neutering or spaying a male, but the kitten soon recovers with no ill effects.

There are many excellent pet shops but few carry pedigree kittens, although they will probably get one for you. Buying from a pet shop does involve the greater risk of infection, as the kitten may well have been in contact with others from unknown homes. Some pet shops will arrange for a kitten to be brought up by a breeder and handed over to the new owner, so that it is not actually taken into the shop. This is an excellent idea.

Buying direct from the breeder is to be recommended, particularly if one can visit the home, see the entire litter and choose the one that has the most appeal. You may also be able to see the mother and appreciate what the grown cat will look like. It is not always possible to see the father as in all probability the mother was sent away to stud. If the variety chosen is in great demand, it may mean ordering a kitten some time in advance.

If unable to find out the names of breeders, *Fur and Feather*, the fortnightly official journal of the Governing Council of the Cat Fancy, carries advertisements giving names and addresses of breeders with kittens for sale.

If given the choice of the litter—it should be at least nine weeks old if you are taking the kitten home with you—choose one that looks bright and gay, with shining eyes wide open, with no dirt or runniness in the corners and with no haws showing. The haw is the third eyelid, which may appear like a skin over the corner of the eye when the kitten or cat is out of condition, or which may be the sign of an illness. The ears should be clean inside, with no smell or discharge—this could mean canker. The nose should feel cool to the touch and appear slightly damp but should not be running. The inside of the mouth should be a healthy pink and the tongue red; if very pale, anaemia may be the cause.

The body should be sturdy and the stomach not hard and distended, perhaps the result of worms or malnutrition. Naturally the fur will not yet have revealed its full length but should be full and fluffy, standing well away from the skin and not clinging or lanky. Blow the fur gently aside to make sure there are not those small black specks in it, which are flea dirts. The little short tail should be held up straight and be clean underneath, with no signs of diarrhoea.

The kitten should be quite steady on its legs, be able to run and play with its litter brothers and sisters. He should show interest in everything that is going on and not run and hide in fright when approached.

If you are not buying for breeding, it is not essential that the kitten should be a show specimen but the breeder should be asked to point out the good and bad points so that you may learn about the breed. If the ears are a little big or the nose too long, the kitten will be just as lovable but, if shown, would lose a few points for such faults. If you intend to show or breed from the kitten eventually, you should say so. It is very unfair for a breeder to sell a kitten that is obviously not up to show standards at a pet price only to visit a show and see it exhibited. It is a very bad advertisement.

Naturally the nearer to the required standards and the better the pedigree, the higher the price. If the kitten has been already shown and won a number of prizes, its value will increase and so will the price. Such a kitten will have outstanding type: small ears, broad head, big round eyes and good chin. The body will be cobby; the legs strong and not too high and the tail short, erect, with no signs of a kink.

The breeder should be asked if the kitten has been inoculated against feline infectious enteritis. If not, this should be done as soon as it has settled in. The veterinary surgeon will recommend a suitable vaccine. Kittens do not suffer from worms to the extent that puppies do but if they are suspected, the vet should be asked for the correct medicine, as more harm is done through wrong treatment than by the worms themselves.

Lastly a word of warning: if, when you visit the breeder to buy a kitten, you find the home looks dirty, the kittens wretched and listless, do not buy—no matter how sorry you feel. You may be buying trouble and having to pay out for vets' bills as well. If there are definite signs that all is not well, the matter should be reported to the local animal welfare society. Unfortunately there are a number of back-yard breeders, as they are called, using cats as mere kitten machines. Usually these kittens are not registered.

## Neutering

Although all breeders and veterinary surgeons recommend neutering of pet cats, many novice cat owners feel it is wrong to deprive a cat of its natural instincts and even talk of 'maiming' the cat. This feeling rarely survives after the cat is adult.

In the case of a queen, if she is let loose when calling, she will disappear for several days, causing anxiety to the family. If she is shut up, the family and neighbours will be kept awake by serenading male cats, who will not only sing for the lady's benefit but will have unholy and ear-shattering fights amongst themselves. This is nature's way of ensuring the survival of the fittest. The courting males will also spray urine around the house and garden, presumably to warn off other males. Male cat urine has to be smelt to be believed and both the smell and the stain are extraordinarily difficult to remove. A female who is not allowed to mate at all becomes frustrated and bad-tempered, loses condition and may even call continuously. In fact she may be so busy calling that she does not have time to stop and eat a proper meal.

In the case of a male cat, when he is adult he will spend more time away from than at home, particularly during the breeding season. He will probably become gaunt and battle-scarred and suffer from many, many abscesses due to fights with other males. If living away from home for any length of time, he stands the chance of being picked up as a stray—perhaps miles from home where he is unlikely to be claimed and so may come to an untimely end.

The female is spayed by ovaro-hysterectomy (the removal of the uterus and ovaries). As the sex hormones are produced by the ovaries, their removal prevents calling, for the spayed female does not have the urge to breed. The mothering instinct, incidentally, does not appear to develop in females that are spayed before their first call though if spayed after having had kittens, some neuter females will mother other cats' kittens but even so, they are still not bothered by the urge to mate. Many neuter females, even those who have previously had kittens, are quite uninterested in other cats' kittens.

In the male, the operation is castration (i.e. both testicles are removed). Within a month the internal male glands will have atrophied and with them the male sexual urge.

To sum up, there appears to be little if anything to be said from the owner's point of view in keeping an entire male. If you live not too near neighbours and like having families of kittens then the entire female is a practical proposition. We are of course left with the thought that if everyone had their pet cats neutered, then there would be no more common or garden kittens!

Both males and females can be neutered from 3½ months up to almost any age. Unless you want your cat to have one or more litters it is best to have her spayed quite young and certainly before the first call. Cats should never be spayed while in season for two reasons. Firstly because the uterus and ovaries are in an active state with engorged blood vessels which entails a larger operation and the added risk of surgical shock. Secondly because it has been known for a female spayed during season to continue calling indefinitely. Have it done between calls, or if she calls unceasingly let her out to be mated and then have her spayed within a fortnight after the mating and when she has stopped calling.

Female kittens practically always take the operation in their stride and frequently astound their owners by returning home after the operation screaming for food. By the next day or so they are completely back to normal and, unless restrained, will be climbing trees and playing wild games. An adult queen takes longer to recover and will not usually eat much until 48 hours after the operation.

Males can be castrated as soon as the testicles have descended from their position in the abdomen and are present in the scrotum. This should normally occur at a very early age but the operation should not take place until after the kitten has been inoculated against feline infectious enteritis. Any lowering of the natural resistance to infection such as even a minor operation is to be avoided. In the case of longhaired cats many people prefer to castrate males over six months old. This is partly so that the broad male head which is an attractive feature of the breed, may develop and also so that the penis may develop. Male cats are fairly prone to cystic calculi (stones in the bladder) which in cats frequently takes the form of fine 'gravel' being formed in the bladder. The larger the penis, obviously the better chance of the cat being able to pass this gravel in the stream of urine, thus preventing blocking of the bladder. This is only a theory and has not been proved but it is obviously worth-while to give this the chance to occur.

Both castrating and spaying can be performed at any age and when cats are no longer required for breeding they can then be neutered and live a happy life as a pet.

You *must* follow your veterinary surgeon's instructions regarding pre- and post-operative care. These will certainly include withholding food prior to the operation and it is no use being soft-hearted and unable to withstand feline demands for breakfast. Food in the stomach increases unnecessarily the anaesthetic risk. (The cat may—more likely will—vomit during the operation, thus causing emergency action to be taken and the consequent interruption of the operation.)

It is important for the cat or kitten to be in good health before neutering. After all, unlike operations which are necessary because of illness requiring surgical treatment, neutering can be peformed at any time and so if you are in any doubt at all consult the surgeon. If a cat or kitten is off colour the stress of the operation may lower the bodily resistance and allow secondary bacterial invaders to multiply, causing serious illness.

The cat or kitten should be presented in a suitable basket or box containing its own blanket. During cold weather a hot-water bottle wrapped in a blanket can be included. Warmth is important after any operation, so do not carry your cat home in a wicker basket with an icy wind whistling through it. The basket should have brown paper or cardboard fastened round the outside to prevent draughts. On the other hand if a box or container is used, make sure that it has sufficient ventilation. Do not use too large a container. For short journeys it is better to have something not too much larger than the occupant. It is very uncomfortable for the cat to be rattled around like a pea in a drum. A few inches clearance all round and sufficient height for it to sit up is quite enough and it is also easier for the owner to carry.

Young kittens need little after care. The male kitten under six months does not require a general anaesthetic and will simply have to be kept reasonably quiet on the day the operation is performed. At the age of six months and onwards a general anaesthetic is required by law and in this case the kitten or adult cat will need longer to recover from the effects of the anaesthetic. Nowadays modern anaesthetics have a short recovery time and most veterinary surgeons probably use a general anaesthetic whatever the age of the kitten.

All that is necessary—and this also applies to all operations—is to keep an eye on the wound in case it should become infected or fail to heal properly.

The female kitten under six months usually makes a quick and uneventful recovery. When she has got over the effects of the anaesthetic the real difficulty is to restrain her from too many acrobatics. If possible she should be prevented from climbing trees or leaping on and off furniture until after the stitches have been removed which is usually in 7–10 days time. Be careful also that she doesn't lick the wound too much. It is not usual to bandage cats after abdominal operations—the wound heals more quickly if exposed to the air—and few cats do more than keep the wound clean. But if licking becomes excessive then she must be bandaged. A pad of gauze or cotton wool should be placed over the wound and kept in place by a firmly, but not tightly, applied *crêpe* bandage.

Adult females mostly spend about two days after the operation quietly resting and during this period should be encouraged to take fluids—solids are not so essential. Of course all cats vary; they wouldn't be cats otherwise and there was the case of an adult queen who went straight home and caught a mouse for her supper!

Because she is lying around and eating less than normal, the queen may become constipated, in which case give her a large teaspoonful of liquid paraffin or olive oil.

Children should not be allowed to lift the cat, nor indeed to pester here in any way during her convalescence. When handling her yourself, lift here 'all in one piece', don't let her hindquarters dangle, thereby putting tension on the muscle wound. After the first day or two, she will gradually return to normal and by the time the stitches are taken out she should be as good as new.

Although a neuter cat will be larger and heavier than the male or female, there is no need for it to become gross. Do not allow it to overeat and see that it takes plenty of exercise. If it is lazy, provide toys such as a ping-pong ball to chase, or a rolled up piece of paper on a string tied to a door handle and hanging just above the height of the cat.

When spaying first became common practice there were

many old wives' tales about it. One, for instance, was that female neuters became blind. All these stories are quite untrue; there is no animal so healthy as a neuter female cat and veterinary surgeons really do themselves a bad turn with every female they spay!

### MONORCHIDS AND CRYPTORCHIDS

An entire male cat should have both testicles correctly placed in the scrotum. If neither are present he is called a cryptorchid and if only one is present he is a monorchid. The missing testicles may be

1. non-existent (a natural neuter)
2. in the groin
3. still in the abdomen

or if a cryptorchid a combination of (2) and (3). A cryptorchid cannot sire kittens, because testicles have to be at less than body temperature to produce spermatozoa—hence their normal position of being carried in a bag outside the body. A monorchid can sire kittens because one testicle is in the correct place but it would be a very unwise breeder who used him at stud.

Monorchidism may be an hereditary condition and it is essential that cats with serious hereditary faults should not be used for breeding. It is only too easy to breed in a defect but it takes many long years of patient work to breed it out.

Cats with either of these faults pass urine with the male smell and also behave as entire males. Castration of a monorchid or cryptorchid is a major operation and may be long and involved. Naturally it is much more expensive than normal castration.

## General care and attention

Longhaired pet cats may be pedigree longhairs which are not up to show standard, half-Persians which are the product of a pedigree queen and the local tom and half-Persians which occur naturally in non-pedigree litters. These presumably have a longhair cat or cats somewhere in their ancestry.

Any of these will, of course, require the same care and attention.

It is very easy to fall in love with an attractive fluffy kitten, whether pedigree or not, but before acquiring it please think carefully if you and your home are suitable for the kitten. Have you got the time and patience required to settle it in its new home and to train it? Will there be someone at home most of the day? It is very unkind to keep a cat where everyone goes out to work all day, leaving it on its own. What a boring life! In any case, should the cat be ill someone will have to be at home to look after it and veterinary surgeons cannot be expected to call out of hours except in case of emergency. Then there are the questions of expense and trouble. Are you prepared for the cost of inoculation and other veterinary fees? Can you afford to feed it properly? These questions apply to any pet animal but in the case of the longhaired cat you must also have time to groom it regularly. If the answer to any of these questions is 'no', then do not have a kitten until circumstances are more favourable.

The kitten should be at least eight weeks old before it leaves its home and preferably 10–12 weeks. Having decided to become the owner of a kitte, the first thing to do is to get a suitable travelling basket or box. There will be many occasions when you have to transport the cat and cats are adept at squeezing out of home-made contraptions. A wicker basket or plastic travelling box is best but adequate cardboard containers can be obtained from the animal welfare societies. It is risky to borrow someone else's basket which has been lent around the neighbourhood. Who knows what infections it may still contain?

Before bringing the kitten home get its bed and sanitary tray ready, so that you can show it these straight away. The bed may be a box or basket with a soft cosy blanket and should if possible be placed under furniture such as a sideboard or table, or else in a corner of the room. Cats like to have cover on all sides to protect them from possible enemies. Once, however, you have provided what looks to be a luxurious and enticing bed, more likely than not the kitten will then decide to sleep somewhere quite different such as on top of the fridge or inside a carrier bag—but its own bed should always be available for it to retreat to.

The sanitary tray should be placed fairly near the bed. Kittens are like babies and need to be potted after waking up and a kitten in a strange home may have forgotten where the tray is if it is not in sight. The tray may contain peat, earth, sand, special litter bought in a pet shop, or even torn-up newspaper. Best to ask the breeder what the kitten has been used to, so that it will recognize the purpose of the tray immediately.

When you bring the kitten home, don't let it run all over the house at first or it will certainly forget where the lavatory is. Keep it confined to the room where you have put its bed and tray and don't forget to close all windows, block the chimney, or put a fire guard in front of an open fire. It will want to explore thoroughly and chimneys are extraordinarily attractive to cats. If you have other pets, introduce the kitten to them gradually and certainly don't leave them alone together until you are sure all is well. There will probably be some swearing to begin with but usually they settle down happily after a few days. Don't, however, forget to make a fuss of the resident animal, who may feel his nose has been put out of joint by the newcomer. Children should not be allowed to handle the kitten too much and should certainly not carry it about. Young children tend to clutch an animal too tightly and if the kitten protests they may drop it. A great many kittens suffer broken legs in this way.

Let the kitten out of doors only under supervision to begin with and only leave him alone in the garden when he has explored it thoroughly and you are sure he knows his way back to the house. From the start the kitten should be trained to come to his meals at the rattle of a dish or a whistle, which is useful for calling him in from the garden.

Practically all kittens are housetrained by their mothers, so provided that he knows where the tray is and he is not shut away from it, there should be little difficulty. It must be kept very clean; cats loathe dirty trays and will go elsewhere rather than use them. If you want your cat to get used to not having a sanitary tray in the house, gradually move the tray nearer to the door until finally it is outside. Many people don't like the idea of a cat tray in the house but personally I think it is better to put up with that than to run the risk of having the cat using any odd corner in the house. Once cats have started to do that it is very difficult, sometimes impossible, to retrain them. There was one black longhair who nearly caused a break-up in her owner's family because she was convinced that the bath was her personal lavatory. Nothing would stop her until the owner hit on the brilliantly simple idea of putting the plug in and always keeping some water in the bath. That did the trick.

When the kitten is older a pophole in the back door of your house is a good idea. This is a hole cut in the door with a flap outside which the cat very quickly learns to push open. These 'cat doors' may be bought from most pet stores. The flap can be bolted shut at night, to keep your cat in and others out. Without a cat door or a small window which can be left open, you will find that much of your time is spent as a cat's commissionaire, for a cat is surely always on the wrong side of a closed door. Of all domestic animals, the cat most values its freedom and a cat which is permanently confined to the house becomes bored and maladjusted and possibly bad-tempered. Cats love to spectate and can spend hours in the garden watching everything that moves. Of course if you live near a road there is always the chance that the cat may meet with an accident but I think better that risk than for it to spend a dreary life cooped up indoors. I lived for many years on a busy main road and the cats not only never went on the road but rarely went to the side of the garden bordering the road. Probably there is more danger from a road with infrequent cars rather than a steady stream of traffic.

Longhaired or half-Persian cats should be groomed every day (see Chapter 10) and at the same time ears, eyes and feet examined for any signs of trouble, such as ear mites, eye infections, ingrowing toe nails, etc.

You will by now, I hope, have given your kitten a name. It is quite surprising how many people, when asked their cat's name say, 'Oh, he doesn't have one, we just call him pussy.' Perhaps they ought to read T. S. Eliot's poem 'The Naming of Cats', in which he recommends that every cat should have three names—an everyday one, a peculiar one which no other cat possesses and a name known only to the cat itself.

When you first get your cat or kitten choose a name as soon as possible and use it repeatedly to begin with, especially when calling him for feeding. He will learn it very quickly. Whether he chooses to answer to it every time you call is another matter and will depend firstly on whether he is hungry; secondly on whether he has more interesting business in hand such as keeping an eye on a mouse-hole; and thirdly on whether he just does not feel like answering at that precise moment. But the more you speak to your cat and communicate with him, the more pleasure you will both get from each other's company. Many people think cats are dull and not as intelligent as dogs but they are generally those who have not lived with a cat, or have not bothered to get to know one. Strangely enough the most fervent cat lovers are often those who rather disliked them before acquiring one.

Kittens should have toys to play with, and indeed so too should adult cats. The conformation, muscle control and reflex actions of the cat are second to none in the animal kingdom, so it is really necessary for kittens to play and exercise with toys in order to develop to their full potential. For example, a table-tennis ball not only gives hours of amusement to the kitten but also speeds up its reflexes because as it is so light it can be batted about at tremendous speed. Of course this darting around—accelerating and slamming on the brakes—also builds up muscles and makes the cat supple. Some sort of soft toy should also be provided which can be tossed in the air and even clutched to the chest and raked with the hindlegs.

A suspended toy is also appreciated. It should be high enough so that the cat has to reach or jump for it. You will soon discover the height your cat prefers. If the toy is on elastic, so much the better because it flies in the air when released and high leaps and twists on the cat's part are required to catch it. Pet shops sell all kinds of toys for cats but as often as not the perverse creature will prefer something simple like an empty cotton reel. Do beware though of plastic toys which can be chewed up or swallowed or may even contain a poisonous substance. Soft toys which can be disembowelled may also be dangerous. I had (and still have) a blue Persian who managed to rip open a catnip mouse and swallow the contents which became jammed in her oesophagus. She choked and was in great distress and in fact was on her way to the operating table when less drastic treatment took effect.

Looking after a kitten is really a matter of common sense and is on similar lines to bringing up children. The young animal needs regular and nourishing meals; plenty of sleep; fresh air; exercise; loving kindness (but not to be smothered in love); and discipline. Avoid over-excitement; excessive handling; over-feeding.

# Feeding

Cats are carnivores and so their diet must contain animal protein and plenty of it. The adult longhair or half-Persian weighing 8–10 lbs needs up to 6 ounces of meat or other protein-rich food and up to 2 ounces of bulk food such as cereal or wholemeal bread divided into two feeds per day. This can only be a generalization, of course, for many cats need much less food and few are likely to require more. Through misplaced kindness pet owners tend to over- rather than under-feed and, like people, some cats are greedy and will eat all that is put before them and ask for more. I knew one woman who literally killed her cats with kindness. She would not believe that they lived for only a few years because of monstrous over-feeding—I shall not mention the amounts she stuffed into her cats every day because no one would believe me if I did!

Cats need a lot of protein, but it does not much matter what form it takes provided you vary it and do not allow the cat to become addicted to one food only, because no one food contains all the necessary nutrients. Unless the diet is varied, the cat can suffer from deficiency diseases. Once a cat has developed a strong preference for, say, fish it is difficult to get it to change its mind. Some cats will almost rather starve than eat anything but the desired food—at least, they will refuse other food for as long as the owner can bear it! I doubt if it has ever been proved that a cat will deliberately starve itself to death but I think it is possible that the cat might refuse food until it loses all desire to eat. I know a great many people say that they only give their cats one particular food such as meat or fish but one usually finds on making further enquiry that the cat also has milk, titbits and access to mice and birds if he needs to make good his deficiencies. If fed on fish only the cat has to eat vast quantities in order to try to meet his nutritional requirements and in time his stomach enlarges and that in turn leads to more eating to fill the gap. So it goes on until the abdominal muscles weaken and sag. Everyone is familiar with the large pear-shaped cat of whose weight and size the owner is tremendously proud—nine times out of ten that cat is a confirmed fish-addict.

Another result of eating too much fish is that some cats develop what is called 'fish eczema'. The first sign of this is that, when looked at from the tail end, the fur down the cat's spine appears sparse. Then the hairs become broken and tiny scabs are formed on the skin. The cat licks and scratches the lesions, which results in moist inflamed patches. Possibly an allergy to fish may also be involved here. Even when the diet is changed, the eczema may take a very long time to clear up—in some cases it never does completely, the cat being plagued with a recurring eczema for the rest of its life.

Deficiency of vitamins, in particular Vitamin A leads to disease and so too does a mineral deficiency. Kittens and young cats are more vulnerable to dietetic deficiencies than are adults and so, from the time of weaning until fully grown, I give Vitamins A and D once daily in the form of Adexolin drops and a mineral supplement called Stress which contains calcium and phosphorus in the correct ratio—a most important point this. There are other proprietary additives, no doubt equally good. Pregnant and nursing queens are also given these supplements.

Starchy foods should always be cooked, as the cat is unable to digest them raw. They are not, in any case, essential to the diet, so do not worry if your cat refuses to eat them, although most cats like at least a small amount and they are useful for adding bulk to the diet.

Fresh drinking water should always be available to the cat, but it is rare for a young healthy cat to drink more than a few laps. Cats mostly rely on the water content of their food to supply their fluid requirements. It is for this reason that I am not in favour of feeding cats an entirely dry food diet. It is foreign to the cat's nature to drink enough to make up for the lack of fluid in the food and I suspect that some cats never would. This could lead to urinary disorders. A small amount of dry food, however, used in emergency or as a snack is quite all right.

As I have said elsewhere, cow's milk is unsuitable for most cats and double-strength dried or evaporated milk is better suited to the cat's digestion.

Here is a list of foods suitable for cats:

*Meat*  Cow beef: either raw or lightly cooked. If cooked, feed the gravy also because it contains the water-soluble vitamins. Horse meat is tolerated by some cats but is often found to be too acid for kittens and nursing mothers.

Liver: raw or cooked; best given only two or three times a week, for it may cause diarrhoea if fed too often.

Tongue and kidney are not universally liked.

Lamb: mostly preferred cooked and preferably roasted.

Melts (spleen): raw or cooked. Give some fat with meaty foods. Most cats will eat only a little. A useful tip given me by a breeder is to throw small pieces of fat to the hungry mob waiting whilst the meat is being cut up. In this way they will eat some while they are hungry, whereas if the fat is given with the food it gets pushed to one side.

Rabbit: cooked. This is top of the pops for the majority of cats. Be careful to remove all bones. This is the ideal food for introducing solids into the small kitten's diet. Mash or chop into small pieces.

Hare: cooked. This is also a favourite.

Chicken: cooked. A great many cats love it. Mine, unfortunately, do not. It is usually the cheapest of the protein foods. Chicken giblets can also be given. If cooked in a pressure cooker or slowly for a long time the neck bones disintegrate and can be mixed up in the feed. Test by squashing between your finger and thumb.

*Fish* Cooked and all bones removed. All white fish is acceptable. Tinned salmon, pilchards, tuna, and sardines are considered delicacies and will often tempt an invalid cat to eat.

*Eggs* Raw or cooked in any way. Egg yolk is a convenient method of increasing the protein content of the diet when required, as for young kittens, nursing queens and convalescent cats.

*Vegetables* Not necessary and not usually liked but no harm comes from giving a little to those who do.

*Cereal* Cornflakes and other breakfast cereals, wholemeal bread (white bread is too 'soggy' to be generally acceptable). Rice or barley cooked in beef or rabbit stock. All these are best fed with meat etc.

*Tinned foods* Cats mostly prefer fresh food and I agree with them. I would not care to live entirely on tinned food myself. However, tins are useful in emergency and if the cat likes them they can be given regularly but I think it advisable that some fresh food be given also.

*Grass*  Opinion is divided on whether this is necessary but certainly all cats like to eat grass at times and so they should have access to it. If you have no garden, grow grass in pots or a window-box. Longhaired cats often eat coarse grass as an emetic in an effort to get rid of fur they have swallowed.

It is best for the cat to be fed at roughly the same time and in the same place each day. They like to regulate their lives and to know when to queue up for meals and they are less likely to pester you for food at other times. Provided the animal is not disturbed while eating—many cats will leave their food instantly if alarmed—remove anything left over and give a smaller feed next time. You may have been overdoing it. On the other hand if the cat clears the dish quickly and looks for more it may need a larger amount—but do not increase the food if the cat is putting on too much weight.

## Special diets

During the breeding season the stud cat will need extra food and so too will the pregnant and nursing queen.

Special diets may be necessary during certain illnesses and your veterinary surgeon will prescribe these.

Aged cats, that is those from 12 years old onwards, usually have excellent appetites. Although quite healthy, they often have a tendency to lose weight and in this case they should have a supplementary feed. If the cat cannot eat any extra food, you may find it will thrive better if the meals are divided into three or even four instead of two per day. The old cat is often more finicky about what it eats, consuming one food ravenously one day and refusing it the next, and I am afraid there is nothing to be done about it but pander to its fancies.

The really old cat—from fifteen on—often requires a greater fluid intake than the young cat, with consequent greater frequency of passing urine. This may be due to chronic nephritis, a common complaint in the old, in which case of course you will have veterinary advice. But quite often the cat is not suffering from any disease so you should not cut down his water supply—he may become dehydrated if you do. It just means you will have to let him out, or clean his sanitary tray, more often.

23 A little Blue-Cream kitten in playful mood. Like children kittens
need toys to keep them amused

24 Cats and dogs can become very close friends

25 An attractive pet, with no pedigree, but bearing a strong resemblance to the Maine Coon cats in the USA

## Holiday care

One of the drawbacks of keeping pets is the problem of what to do with them when you go on holiday. As far as the cat is concerned, probably the best solution is for a neighbour to feed and look after him in his own home. He must of course have access to the house by a cat-flap in the door, or to a dry, draught-free garden shed to sleep in. Two to three weeks is really the limit to leave him like this, less than that for the first time. After this period cats have often been known to leave home, apparently giving up hope of their owner's return. Ideally, the neighbour would spend a little time with the cat, chatting to him and looking him over to see that he is in good health and possibly grooming him. Another possibility is for a friend to have him in her own home, so for the first few days at least he would have to be confined.

On occasion you may be able to take the cat with you, for instance if you are caravanning or renting a seaside bungalow. But not all cats take kindly to this arrangement and you will need to have some idea of how he will behave or you may find your holiday ruined. A timid or nervous cat may easily panic and get lost in strange surroundings and many cats do not enjoy travelling.

## Boarding catteries

If you cannot make any of these arrangements then you will have to send him to a boarding cattery. Make your booking well in advance, especially in summer time, because the cattery will be unlikely to be able to accommodate him at the last moment. Perhaps a friend or your veterinary surgeon can recommend a good place but in any case you should visit the cattery yourself, both to inspect the accommodation and to find out what is required on your part. More than likely the cattery will want you to produce a certificate to show that your cat has been inoculated against feline infectious enteritis within the last year. Make an appointment to see the place; do not turn up expecting to be shown round immediately. This does not mean that the cattery has anything to hide but it is not always convenient to show visitors round—at feeding time, for instance, when you would disturb the cats. Beware of catteries whose charges are much lower than anywhere else. You get what you pay for and running a cattery is quite a costly business, so that if the charges are too cheap it might mean that your cat is not very well looked after and gets poor quality food.

When you go to see a boarding cattery you should first make sure it is clean. There must be no dirty food dishes lying around or sanitary trays which have obviously not been cleaned for some time. The housing must be adequate with sufficient space for each cat, an outdoor run of its own and no direct contact with other cats. If it is winter time a safe source of heat should be available for a cat who is accustomed to sleep indoors. The attitude of the owner and staff to the cats is also important. The homesick cat will only settle down and eat well if looked after by people who are sympathetic towards and understand cats. After all, the animal has no means of telling, the first time it is boarded out, that it is ever going to see its home and owners again. So it is understandable that it will take a day or two to adjust itself and during that time kindness and understanding from the attendant are essential.

Most catteries will allow you to bring the cat's own blanket, which will help to make him feel at home. You should also leave:

1. A list of his favourite foods—though what usually happens is that the cat will eat everything else but those foods, being the contrary creature it is.

2. Your holiday address and telephone number. If you cannot be contacted on holiday, then leave the name, address and telephone number of a relation or friend authorized to make any decisions regarding the cat.

3. The name, address and telephone number of your veterinary surgeon if he is to attend the cat should it be ill. Let your veterinary surgeon know that the cat is in a boarding cattery and, if you cannot be contacted while away, then I suggest that you give him permission in advance to do whatever he thinks necessary—an X-ray, operation or, at the worst, to put the cat to sleep. This may sound pessimistic but it so often happens that an animal is taken ill while the owner is away and, while a veterinary surgeon will take the responsibility for carrying out essential treatment, it is better for all parties that it should be agreed in advance.

You may have difficulty in finding a cattery which will

board a full male, a female in season, or a young kitten. I also do not know of any cattery or hospital which will take a cat suffering from an infectious illness, so if you have the bad luck to have your cat succumb to one of these just before you go away, you will either have to arrange for a friend to look after it or give up your holiday.

TRAVEL

It is very unsafe to travel with a cat loose in the car. Apart from the obvious risk of it jumping on the driver's lap and distracting him, it is very easy to forget the cat is there and to open a window—and out goes the cat.

Most cats are reasonable, if sometimes noisy, travelling companions but quite a few hate journeys and work themselves up into a state of near panic. Sedatives are not really very helpful, quite often having little effect on cats except to cause them to lose balance. It may help if you first take the cat on very short journeys, gradually getting it accustomed to longer distances. Some cats travel better if they can see where they are going, others prefer not to—so it may be worth-while trying both ways.

There are various types of travelling baskets or boxes, some of them transparent. Whatever type you use be sure there is plenty of ventilation, though draughts must be avoided. Do not forget to put in a blanket or thick wad of newspaper, especially in the basket type. It always makes me shudder when a basket is opened and there is the cat sitting uncomfortably on the wickerwork. It is not advisable to put food or drink in the basket, it only gets spilt and if the cat is fed properly before the journey it will not need it.

## Behaviour and intelligence

It is not rational to try to assess the intelligence of the cat by comparing it with the dog, when the behaviour pattern of the two animals is so different, particularly in relation to man. Anyway there is really no reason to want them to behave in a similar manner.

It is fairly easy to train a dog to perform an action on command for which he does not see the reason but does it in order to please his owner. The cat, however (with few exceptions), will not perform boring and repetitive tricks simply to obey his owner. But if a certain action brings about something to the cat's advantage, then he will quickly learn how to perform it. For instance, there is usually no trouble in teaching a cat to use a cat-flap door, because by doing so he can come and go as he pleases. Therefore if the assessment of intelligence is based on the ability to learn, the cat must have a reasonably high IQ.

Differentiating between instinct and intelligence can be difficult. A lost cat may use its homing instinct to return to its home but should it not be able to do so, perhaps because of distance, then after the initial period of shock and bewilderment it is capable of adapting itself to its environment. In a town or village it will rely on people's kindness for most of its food, finding sleeping quarters in a convenient shed. With any luck it may find someone to adopt it. In the country it will probably revert completely to a wild life, hunting its food and sleeping rough. It might be fair to say that one measure of intelligence is the ability to use instinct in a practical manner.

The behaviour of cats is a fascinating study. Although cats are supreme individualists, general patterns of behaviour can be seen. They have a strongly developed territorial sense, chasing off any strange cats who dare to trespass. They mark out their territory by spraying urine at intervals round the bounds and this is done not only by male cats but by queens and neuters too. When moving house with his owners a cat usually has a rough time in the new district from the resident cat population until he establishes his own territory. This is one very good reason for keeping your cat confined and taken in the garden only under supervision until he is completely acclimatized. If he becomes involved in a fight as soon as he arrives at his new home, he may be chased away for a considerable distance and be unable to find his way back, or be too frightened to attempt it.

Another trait that all cats have in common is that they are independent. They are not particularly anxious to please and in the main do not like to be picked up and fussed over unless they should happen to be in the mood for it. On the other hand, the time that they pick to want to sit on your knee is more than likely to be highly inconvenient to you, almost as if that moment were chosen on purpose. They can certainly be very perverse:

a good example of this is that a visitor who does not love cats is likely to be the object of an unwanted show of affection from the cat. Unless restrained, the cat will jump on his or her lap with loud purrs, demanding attention and apparently oblivious to the fact that it is not welcome.

Probably the most outstanding cat characteristic is their curiosity. A strange place has to be explored thoroughly and any uncommon object or noise investigated. This very often leads to trouble for the cat because they climb up chimneys and are unable to get down again, get shut in cupboards or garden sheds, while many have been carried away in cars or delivery vans which they had crept into unseen. No doubt this attribute gave rise to the saying: 'curiosity killed the cat' and 'a cat has nine lives'—the latter because the cat so often survives catastrophes and accidents brought about by its prying habits.

All cats dislike loud clattering noises, and this may be partly due to their acute hearing. A noise which does not sound too bad to us may be unbearable to the cat's ears. Sudden movements are always viewed with suspicion, so if you want to approach a cat, do so slowly and quietly, otherwise it will simply run away.

Individual cats all have their own behaviour patterns and the observant owner will quickly learn to understand them. This is helpful because a change of behaviour can be an early indication that there is something wrong with the cat. To put it simply, if a cat that normally likes to spend most of its time outdoors is seen to be lying about sleeping all day, then more than likely it is not feeling well and should be examined for any signs of illness.

Whether or not cats can see colours I do not know but they can certainly differentiate betwen dark and light colours. I have always had difficulty in getting my chinchillas to fraternize with either blacks or blues, and *vice versa*. There is either a state of armed neutrality or even open warfare.

Cats will often have a special friend, or live quite happily in small groups, but they never do well kept in large packs. Breeding problems arise, as do skin troubles and respiratory infections and the cats rarely appear healthy and happy.

Another common characteristic is that of taking a fancy to a particular sleeping place. This fancy may last for days or weeks but is not usually permanent, except in the case of the very old cat who mostly adopts a special spot. These fancied places do not always look very attractive to the human eye as, apart from a bed or a chair, they may be on top of a piece of furniture, on a window sill, inside a paper bag, on the stairs— or any other unlikely site. The one place which is always popular with my cats in winter is the mat in front of the Aga cooker, because of the constant warmth. I am now quite accustomed to cooking at arm's length and being specially careful not to spill.

Some cats are intrigued by water and will spend hours watching a dripping tap, trying to catch the drops. A few will swim but, apart from the Turkish cats, this is rather rare in longhairs. If you keep fish, either in a tank or in a pond in the garden, you will have to see that it is cat-proof, or that there is sufficient depth of water for the fish to escape from the lightning paw of a feline angler.

Apart from cleansing its coat, the cat uses the action of grooming for other purposes. A quick lick of the bib will cover up a moment of embarrassment and when two enemy cats confront each other the cat that intends to give way will often sit down and groom itself as a sign of submission.

Most cats are sticklers for routine and their movements form a set pattern. Usually I have a fair idea of where to find my cats at any particular time of day, although they run completely free. When I let them out in the morning, each cat carries out her habitual action. One always rushes to an old tree trunk and strops her claws, another has a bite of grass, a third goes to sit in a particular spot to survey the garden—and so on.

Cats like meals to appear at the same time and in the same place every day. Change the feeding place and the cat is immediately suspicious and takes a little time to settle to its food; some even refuse to eat unless the dish is put in its normal place.

It would be interesting to know why catmint causes such extraordinary behaviour in cats. Some will sniff it and sneeze, rather like a person taking snuff. Others rub their heads in it then go and roll about in ecstasy and some stamp and roll on the actual plant, pounding it into the ground. The plant does not seem to be attractive all the time, whether in flower or not, but I have noticed that when I have been weeding around the catmint, the cats are always attracted to it. So it may be that when the stems or leaves are bruised they give off a particular scent.

By observing the cat's behaviour pattern the owner can learn to interpret its needs and is therefore able to communicate with it to a certain extent. Facial expression, voice and posture are all used by the cat to convey its meaning to an interested person. The voice of a mother cat chatting to her kittens is quite different from the voice she uses to demand food and certainly a far cry from the sounds made by two tomcats fighting. The cat also uses its ears and tail to 'speak' to its owner. For instance, if you call the cat when it has its back to you and it turns one ear down and sideways, this usually means 'I hear you but am too busy to come just at the moment.' Similarly, the tail is used as a signal. If you call the cat when it is walking and it immediately raises its tail straight up this means 'I am willing to speak/come to you/be lifted up.' If the tail is not hoisted this means 'I do not wish to be stopped, catch me if you can.' These are just a few examples—every cat will have its own expressions and actions which form a fascinating study for humans.

## Care of the old cat

Nowadays the average life-span of the cat is much greater than it was even 20 years ago. At that time 12–13 years was considered really old but now it is quite common to see 16–18-year-old cats enjoying a reasonably active life. I think this is partly due to more enlightened ideas on feeding, at least as far as the pet cat is concerned. At one time people tended to think a cat could live on table scraps and anything it could catch. Modern drugs have also played a great part in prolonging life.

While still preserving its independence, the old cat will require more care and vigilance from the owner in various ways.

As the cat ages, so it loses much of its subcutaneous fat and therefore needs to live in a warm atmosphere. In winter, many old cats never set foot outside, except perhaps on a sunny day, being content to snooze most of the time. The longhaired cat can tolerate dry cold reasonably well but you must be careful not to leave an old cat shut outdoors for too long in damp or wet weather. The coat insulates the cat by trapping air between the hairs and if the coat becomes damp or wet so its insulating property is destroyed and old cats get chilled easily.

Teeth should be inspected regularly. A deposit of tartar on the teeth is very common and this needs to be removed, otherwise the gums recede and become infected. Bad teeth will have to be extracted but this is not a serious matter—a cat can manage very well with no teeth at all, provided its food is cut into bite-sized pieces.

Hearing and sight usually remain good, although not so acute as when the cat was in its prime. If the cat should become affected in either of these senses, then it must be protected from attack by dogs or other cats and certainly traffic hazards. In other words, such a cat should not be allowed to roam freely. This is quite different from the case of the congenitally deaf cat. I had a deaf white cat who lived a natural life until old age and, never having been able to hear, she used her other senses more to compensate and was particularly sensitive to vibrations. The aged cat (and any other animal) which becomes deaf appears to think that because it can no longer hear a dangerous noise, such as traffic, then that danger no longer exists. If, however, it is the sight which is affected it will, to a certain extent, use its hearing, touch, sense of smell to guide it.

As the cat grows older, more thought will have to be given to diet. Most probably it will prefer to have its daily ration in three or four small meals rather than in two large ones. Usually also the fluid intake increases with age and it may like either to have drinks of gravy or milk or to have its food fairly sloppy. Sometimes too the cat becomes more fastidious and what it will eat ravenously one day will be refused the next. So you will have to think up as varied a diet as possible.

As the animal's body grows older, the digestive processes slow down and become less efficient and therefore food should be of good quality and as nutritious as possible. It may be found necessary to give a bulk laxative such as 'Normacol' or 'Isogel' two or three times a week if the cat tends to be constipated. This often happens in old age because peristalsis (the rhythmic contractions which enable the bowel contents to pass along the intestinal tract) slows down and the rectum becomes packed with faeces which the cat is unable to expel. Adding bulk to the diet may help to stimulate the bowel wall to contract.

As many aged cats cannot always be bothered to go outside to dig a hole, you will probably have to spend more time cleaning the sanitary tray.

The longhaired cat does not usually grow such a profuse coat when it is really old as it did when it was younger but it will need just as much, if not more, grooming, especially if it has lost some of its front teeth. The coat loses some of its vitality and the cat will need your help to get rid of the dead hair and to keep the coat clean. Be very gentle in grooming the elderly cat because, having lost some of its subcutaneous fat, the cat does not like to feel the comb rattling on its ribs.

To make up for all the extra work and time involved in looking after the old-age pensioner, you will generally find that the old cat has developed greatly in character and is an even more charming and affectionate companion than when it was young and independent.

# Chapter four

# Breeding

## The queen

From the time of mating until weaning the welfare of the kittens depends almost entirely on the queen, who in turn is dependent on her owner for a supply of good food and for suitable conditions in which to produce and rear her litter.

So before embarking on cat breeding, pause to consider whether you have the time to spare to cope with the kittening and the weaning of the kittens. More than likely the queen will require no more than your availability during the actual birth, managing it all herself. But you must take all eventualities into account and things may go badly wrong so that your constant presence and help will be needed. If a caesarian section, for example, has to be performed you may, at worst, have to devote several days to nursing the queen and kittens and even hand-rearing the kittens. Although kittens are usually quite easily weaned, a certain amount of time has also to be set aside for preparing their food and serving it to them at frequent and regular intervals.

Then there is the question of suitable quarters, whether in your own house or in a cat house. The room where the kittening is to take place and where the cat and her kittens will live for the first two or three weeks should be well-ventilated but not draughty. Have a source of heating which can keep the room at the required temperature without over-heating the cat and is readily adjustable. You will also need adequate lighting, both natural and artificial.

Having decided that you are able and willing to look after a breeding queen then buy as well-bred a kitten or cat as you can obtain. If you want to show as well as breed, she should also be good-looking, but the quality of her kittens will depend on her ancestors as well as herself. (This also applies to the male cat.) It is important too that she should be a healthy, well-grown kitten and if possible come from a line of fertile females with a record of trouble-free parturition.

While she is a kitten, the breeding female should lead a natural cat's life with ample freedom and exercise so that she can develop her muscles and physique and will thus be in good hard condition when it is time for her to be mated. She must also have a balanced and adequate diet while she is developing, with the addition of minerals and vitamins.

Character and temperament must not be forgotten and it is during kittenhood and adolescence that the breeding female can be most in the owner's company and live with the family while these traits are developing. There is a parallel here with the case of working dogs such as those being trained to be guide dogs for the blind, who spend their puppyhood with a carefully chosen family and not confined to kennels.

The queen who has had a happy, carefree kittenhood and who has come to know and trust her people is the one who will grow up into a well-balanced, self-reliant individual likely to take the whole business of kittening and motherhood in her stride. But if trouble arises, she will know that she can rely on her owner for help, having built up an understanding in her early days.

## The stud

Many novices think that the correct way to start breeding is to buy a pair of unrelated male and female kittens who when they are old enough will mate and produce litters which may be sold for large sums but it is just not practicable to start with one of each sex. Cats mature at different ages, even if of the same varieties, and a female will probably be ready for mating before the male has fully matured. The longhairs develop later than the Siamese and other shorthairs and a male may not reach maturity until he is 12 months or more. In some cases it could even be two years before he mates his first queen. A female may start calling, that is, come into season, when about seven or eight months, although she should not be mated until ten or eleven months at least, and then only if she has already called once and is fully grown.

It may be the other way about: the male develops faster than the female. He may attempt to mate her before she is fully ready and she may turn on him, making him feel that he should beware of any other female cats he meets, attacking them before they go for him. A fully developed female may keep worrying a too young male, turning spiteful when he fails to mate her— this could spoil her for future breeding. It also happens, when they live together all the time, that they are so used to one another that the male will ignore the female completely when she is in season, although he will mate any other female.

Most fanciers start by buying one or two females and sending them away to stud, for taking on a male cat needs most careful consideration. There are both advantages and disadvantages.

The advantage is that there is not the bother of sending the queens away. Many stop calling when taken to a stud— particularly if it is the first time—and have to go back. Some females do not take and may have to return. With today's heavy travelling costs the saving can be considerable if one has one's own male on hand—time is saved too.

Some of the most successful breeders own their own stud, finding the queens can be put in with the male as soon as they are ready and avoid the upset of travelling.

The disadvantages are that, unless you intend to have three or four queens, it will be necessary to have visiting females to keep him happy, with the risk of introducing infection, and you have to use the same stud each time and every litter will not be outstanding. However good both the male and the female may be, they do not always suit one another and the kittens they produce may always be pet, instead of champion standard. I had a stud of champion standard who, mated to my outstanding queens, never produced anything but mediocre kittens—from a show point of view. They were strong healthy attractive kittens, however, and certainly made delightful pets with wonderful temperaments.

A further disadvantage is that it is rarely possible for a male stud to have complete freedom. Many unneutered mongrel pets come and go as they please but they usually advertise their presence in the house by their unpleasant pungent smell. They are often away for days, chasing and mating female cats, coming home with ears torn and other injuries, looking bedraggled and often starving. It is unfortunate that for these reasons the pedigree stud does have to live a great deal of his life alone.

It is unfair to buy a male kitten, bring him up as pet and then shut him up in a house all on his own where he can see very little activity. If bought as a future stud, he should be introduced, when a few months old, to his house and allowed to sleep in it until he gradually becomes used to a restricted life. Even if a large run is provided—it should be if at all possible— he should, when eventually he lives in the house all the time, be allowed daily exercise and play in the garden under his owner's eye. His house should also be so sited that he can see people coming and going and can be talked to frequently. A stud that is left alone a great deal may become restless, unhappy and frequently noisy, complaining bitterly. Studs are usually very affectionate and friendly, loving attention.

The male chosen as a future stud should be a good example of his variety and as near to the set standard as possible. The breeder from whom he is purchased should be told that it is hoped that he will become a future stud, as this will be a good advertisement for her should he sire good kittens.

If he is to be at public stud he should be exhibited so that he may be seen by the owners of queens for them to consider his possibilities as a future mate for the queens. If he does become a champion, there will certainly be many wishing to use him to improve their stock and also in the hope of breeding prize-winning kittens. There is the danger that he may be over-used and, however tempting may be the thought of some extra money, a wise stud owner always puts his male's physical well-being before anything else and restricts the number of matings.

Keeping a successful stud not only depends on the male's capabilities but has also a great deal to do with the owner. Time and patience are essential as all matings have to be supervised and this may mean spending many hours in the stud's house.

The house provided should be large enough for the owner to stand up in. There should be a separate wired-off section for the visiting queens to sleep in, where she is able to see the male without coming into contact except through the wire. All the surfaces in the house should be washable and shelves should be provided for the male to get onto out of the queen's way once mated. A piece of old carpet, which can be washed, should be put on the floor during the mating to provide a foothold. Windows too are important as the house must be light and airy. There should be a flap for the male to get into his run and this should be closed when he has a queen to prevent any possible escapes.

The outside run must be as large as possible, part grass—for chewing—and part concrete—for easy washing down. There should be tree stumps or posts for scratching on and boxes or planks for climbing and exercising on. Playthings such as balls, should also be provided. The stud house should not be too near that of neighbours, as females when mated often utter very loud screams; a male too may caterwaul in the middle of the night, with complaints soon following regarding the noise. Some males too may spray in their houses and, no matter how often the houses are washed down with disinfectant, the tomcat smell is very persistent.

Only queens inoculated against feline infectious enteritis should be accepted and each visitor should be carefully inspected for fleas, dirty ears or any other illness, before being put in the separate compartment in the stud's house. They should be allowed to become acquainted with one another without actually being in physical contact until it is evident by her little cries and rollings that she is ready for mating. A maiden queen may be difficult. She may be frightened at being away from her home for the first time and so shy that she disappears into her quarters for hours. She should be left until she makes up her mind to emerge. Probably the male will then start crooning to her through the wire, calming her down.

When ready to be mated, she will crouch in front of him, when he will jump on her back, holding her by the loose skin in the nape of the neck. Immediately a successful mating has taken place, the queen will probably start shrieking loudly, hitting out at the male who will jump onto the nearest shelf out of her way. She will roll around for a few minutes and then start washing herself. As soon as she can be handled she should be put back in her compartment. The male too will start washing himself. After a few hours another mating should be given. The female should not be sent back immediately but preferably returned the next day, having had time to sleep and eat in the meantime. The owner should be contacted before she is sent back to ensure that she can be met, if being sent by train.

The stud fee is payable in advance and if the first visit does not produce kittens, the queen may be taken for a further mating but this is entirely at the stud owner's discretion and is not compulsory. A copy of the male's pedigree with the date of the stud service should be given or sent to the owner of the female, as she will need it to issue the pedigrees for the kittens and to register them. The house must then be thoroughly cleaned out before the next queen is accepted.

Stud work is not an easy way to make money. Queens often resent coming for a mating and frequently those the owners declare are most docile will hit out when first handled if care is not taken.

The stud's feeding is all important if he is to stay in first-class condition and sire strong healthy kittens. Raw meat is absolutely essential in the diet, with variety provided (see Feeding). His drinking water must be changed daily. Regular grooming is essential with watch being kept in case a stray flea has been picked up from a visitor and his ears inspected as he may catch canker from one of them.

During the breeding season a male does tend to lose weight but he should put this on again during the winter. Some breeders allow one of the females or a neuter to live with him as a companion when there are no visitors; this does help to make him less lonely.

## The oestrus cycle

Longhairs seldom come in season or 'call' before the age of six months and mostly at about nine to ten months. There is no hard and fast rule for the age at which cats should be bred. This will depend entirely on the maturity and physical condition of the individual, bearing in mind that the ideal would be for the queen to have her first litter at around one year old and preferably in the spring or early summer so that the growing kittens will have the benefit of sunlight. In any case the queen should not be mated at her first call. Coming into season is a new experience to which the queen has to adjust herself and she should not at this time have the added stress of leaving home to visit a stud cat as well.

If the female comes into season at an early age and continues to call at frequent intervals, then it is less harmful to mate her than to hold her back for too long. Cats who are frustrated by being prevented from mating for too many seasons are subsequently found to be difficult if not impossible to get in kitten. If you are in doubt about mating a young queen, your veterinary surgeon will tell you whether she is mature and healthy enough to rear a family.

There is only one sure thing about the feline oestrus cycle and that is that individuals will vary from each other both in frequency and duration of season. In this, as in everything else, the cat is an individualist. The general rule for longhairs is that the breeding season starts in January and continues until late autumn but of course there are many exceptions. Weather appears to influence the onset of oestrus and in mild winters I have had queens calling at Christmas time. Even if mated then, they are not likely to conceive. A spell of cold weather in January and February can result in a later start to the breeding season.

The length of the call is variable and some queens, if not mated, will continue to call for weeks. Or even if mating has taken place but has not stimulated ovulation then the call may continue for a considerable time. The average duration is 5–7 days if not mated and it is usually considered that mating is most likely to be successful on the third to fourth day. The queen should be sent to stud on the second day, always provided that her call is well-established, otherwise the stress of the journey may put her off.

While the frequency of oestrus varies in cats as a whole, the individual female is likely to call at approximately the same intervals during the breeding season and these may be anything from 7 to 28 days. Once established, her oestral pattern is likely to be repeated in subsequent years. Some queens may only call once or twice in the whole season and these are not usually good breeders.

SIGNS OF OESTRUS

The first evidence is usually increased friendliness on the cat's part, shown by rubbing against the owner's legs and generally wanting to be fussed over. She will also be restless, prowling

26  Motherhood: a Birman nursing her beautiful quadruplets

27  Where's that other kitten? A Bi-Colour trying to find out

28 Young Blue kittens just learning to lap

29 The hunting instinct is strong in some cats as shown by this Black kitten

round the house and often jumping on the window-sill to look out—no doubt to see if any males are around. As a matter of fact, even before the queen has shown any inclination to call, you should be on your guard if you see a tomcat in your garden. These roaming males know where every female lives and appear to find her attractive before she is really calling. What is more, once having located her, they seem to keep a mental diary and will arrive every time she is due, unless they are otherwise engaged. Nor do they forget during the period of anoestrus, which is roughly September till January, and may be expected to turn up on time the following year.

At the time she becomes restless the queen's voice will alter and she will utter loud imperious cries, quite unlike her normal voice. So much so that one wonders how the voice that is usually heard as a melodious mew can be so transformed. She will also cast herself on the ground and roll violently from side to side on her back. At this stage I have often been sent for by pet owners because they do not realize what is happening and believe the cat to be in great pain. Indeed it is frequently their first intimation that the kitten they were given as a male is in fact a female.

When the female is ready to accept the male she will crouch on the floor with her hindquarters raised, 'marking time' with her back legs and often crooning to herself.

When the queen is expected to come in season, or at the latest as soon as there is any alteration in her behaviour, she should be confined to the cattery or, if a house cat, shut in one room—make sure that the chimney is blocked and all windows closed or with escape-proof grids on them. Lock the door or hang a notice on it to remind other people that it must be kept closed. A word of warning about confining a calling queen in an outside cat house may save you complaints from neighbours: your cat house is liable to become the Mecca for tomcats from far and wide and if you have neighbours within 100 yards they (and you) will get no sleep because of the constant caterwauling. It is also very frustrating for your queen to be so near the males and yet unable to get to them and so she is better shut up out of sight and sound if this is possible.

The maiden queen, although her instinct prompts her to go and seek a mate, possibly will not be so adept at escaping as an experienced queen. I have had cats who have been cunning

G

enough to suppress all signs of coming into heat and, if I have not been expecting it, my first inkling might be the sight of a feline figure gambolling in the garden and calling loudly for the local tomcat.

Long before the queen is likely to call, you must decide which stud cat you want to send her to and arrange matters with his owner. You will not of course be able to give a definite date for her visit. If you are a novice you will probably find it worthwhile to ask advice from the breeder of your cat about the choice of a suitable mate. I have always found that people in the Cat Fancy are kind and helpful to newcomers. Or if you prefer to choose the stud yourself then attend as many cat shows as you can and spend some time studying the male cats and their pedigrees and any progeny that may be present. Do not use a cat too closely related to your queen. Experienced breeders practice line-breeding and inbreeding but this is not for the novice. Mating closely related animals fixes the bad points as well as the good ones and faults so introduced are difficult to eradicate from a strain. Naturally you will want to breed as good kittens as possible. Therefore you must be honest enough to acknowledge (if only to yourself) your female's weak points and look for a male without similar faults—no cat is perfect so even a grand champion is likely to have some fault however slight. For instance, if your queen has rather large ears, then it is only sensible to choose a male with neat ears.

THE JOURNEY

It is really much more satisfactory if you can take a maiden queen to stud rather than send her off on her own. The strain of a solitary journey can quite easily put her off call, or if she does mate, she may be so upset that she fails to conceive. If you can accompany her and settle her in her quarters, a successful mating is far more likely. At the same time it gives you a chance to satisfy yourself about the conditions under which your queen will be kept.

Never send your cat off by train to an unknown stud owner, for you can have no idea what the place will be like or how she will be treated. If you have not met the stud owner, ask someone in the cat world for advice before making any arrangements.

As soon as your queen shows signs of coming into season at

the time when you propose to have her mated, contact the stud owner and fix which day she shall travel and if going by train say at what time she will arrive.

Unless it is absolutely necessary, do not send a cat on a rail journey which entails changing trains. It has happened that a cat has been mislaid, delayed, or even put on the wrong train. This is most distressing for the cat and all the people concerned and prolongs the travelling for many unnecessary hours. Far better to take her to a station from which she goes direct to the station at which she can be met by the stud owner.

The travelling basket or box should be strong, escape-proof, well-ventilated and contain a warm blanket. Do not use a cardboard container, because a frightened cat can easily rip this to pieces and escape. If a box or fibreglass container is used, there should be ventilation on more than one side in case the apertures are blocked during travel by other luggage. A wicker basket should have brown paper fixed round the sides in all but the hottest weather, otherwise it will be draughty.

The box should be big enough for the cat to lie comfortably, turn round and stand up but not so large that she is thrown about in it during the journey. I would say that a box measuring 18″ × 12″ × 12″ is the minimum size for a small-to-medium longhair queen. A massive queen will of course need a larger box. Whether you use box or basket, make sure that it is clearly labelled with the stud owner's name, address and telephone number; a livestock label; and details of the journey such as the stations of departure and destination, time of train and marked 'to be called for'. Inside the container fix a label with your own name, address and telephone number, both so that you can be contacted in case of emergency and which can be used by the stud owner on the return journey.

When the queen comes back from stud, she must be confined for some days until you are quite sure she has stopped calling. Because cats do not ovulate for up to 30 hours after they have been mated, it is quite possible for a queen to be mated by different males and to have a litter containing kittens sired by different fathers. In the natural state a female cat may be mated 25–30 times during one heat, so it is not surprising that queens miss when sent to stud, where they only have two or three matings. This is a problem of pedigree cat breeding to which I see no immediate solution. Naturally stud owners cannot allow their males to mate every visiting queen all day long: the cat would be worn out before the end of the breeding season. But I do think each queen should have a minimum of three matings, spread over a period of at least 24 hours. It should not be overlooked that the more queens that become pregnant from their first visit the fewer will be returned to stud having failed to conceive. So more matings per queen would not necessarily increase a virile stud cat's work.

Unlike bitches, which may be mated shortly after being taken to the dog, a queen will have to be left for a few days, given time to settle down and then mated. If no kittens result from the first visit, she may be accepted again. If there is a return visit, travelling expenses and her food should be paid for.

## The pregnant queen

### GESTATION PERIOD

At one time it was thought that 63 days was the average gestation period of the cat but, certainly in longhairs, it appears now that 65 days is more accurate and in many cases 67–69 days is quite usual. This fits in with the fact that kittens born before the 61st day seldom survive and if the gestation period were really 63 days, for them to be born two days early would not be unduly premature. As soon as you know the dates of mating, calculate when the kittens will be due and arrange your life accordingly, not making any engagements for several days before and after the estimated time of arrival. Most veterinary surgeons appreciate being given dates of expected kittening so that work may be arranged accordingly. Don't forget to let him know when the kittens have arrived, if you have not required his help.

### CARE

For the first few weeks the queen does not require special care and the more nomal a life she can lead the better. If she has previously been allowed her freedom, then she should still be free—always watching for any sign of calling, in case she should not be pregnant. She will not need any extra food at this stage and if she is kept in a cattery must be encouraged to take plenty of exercise. Sitting around in a cat house is no preparation for parturition. As those of you who have had babies will remember the act of giving birth is a strenuous and exhausting business and so the aim should be to have the queen in as hard muscular condition as possible. Check the queen for internal or external parasites, and if you have not wormed her before mating she should have a roundworm dose during the first fortnight of pregnancy.

At 3–4 weeks, if it is necessary for you to know if the queen is in kitten, a pregnancy diagnosis can be carried out by a veterinary surgeon. On no account should the owner keep prodding the cat's abdomen to feel the kittens—or indeed at any stage. Damage to the foetus can easily be caused in this way.

Towards the fourth week the queen's teats will alter, becoming enlarged and rosy pink in colour and from now on she will change bodily, becoming gradually pear-shaped. The size of her abdomen has little relation to the number of kittens she is carrying. She may look as if she were going to have a baker's dozen and only produce two or three kittens while the queen who looked comparatively slim may have five or six.

From the fifth week, her diet should be supplemented with Vitamins A and D and minerals, especially calcium. Lack of these additives can result in kittens being born with open eyes and cleft palates. If the queen is hungry, the amount of food can now be increased—by how much will depend on the individual. This is best done by giving extra feeds rather than a greater amount at one time but do be careful not to overfeed. She will need plenty of protein-rich foods but any increase in fattening foods should be avoided. A fat flabby queen is a likely candidate for kittening problems.

About a fortnight before the kittening date, prepare the box in which you intend the kittens to be born. Quite likely the queen will have other ideas and at this time she will be prospecting for attractive kittening places and so the doors of all cupboards and wardrobes should be kept closed as these are favourite nesting places. The most suitable place for the kittening box to be situated is the one which is most convenient for you and acceptable to the cat, always provided that it is out of draughts and that heating is available as required.

Personally I like to have the kittening take place in my bedroom, so many queens seem to have their kittens during the night and if the box is in my room I merely have to switch on the light to check progress. In any case I like to look at the queen at least once nightly when the birth is imminent. If the idea of having a kittening in your bedroom does not appeal to you, then I would recommend that at least it takes place under your roof. It is no fun at all to have to go outside several times on a wet night to a cat house or a garden shed. In any case most cats like to know that their owner is nearby and this applies particularly to maiden queens.

The actual box should be large enough for the cat to be able to stretch out. It should have three high sides with the fourth side only about six inches high, to enable the mother to get in easily but to confine the young kittens. For bedding I use a thick pile of newspapers, the top layer being removed as it becomes soiled or torn. As the kittening date draws near, the queen will probably make her nest many many times, tearing up quantities of paper. Blankets as bedding can be dangerous because it is quite possible for a very young kitten to crawl into a fold of blanket and be unable to find its way out. If this should happen during the night it could be many hours before it was found. If you do use a blanket, the ends must be carefully tucked in or fastened down so that this is not likely to happen. During the kittening and for a week or two after I drape a blanket over the high sides of the box, because cats generally like a shaded place in which to have their kittens and because kittens' newly opened eyes require time to adjust to full daylight.

From the seventh week the kittens become increasingly active. Their movements may be felt by laying a hand gently on the mother's abdomen. Later on, rippling movements can be seen as well as felt. Some queens look sharply at their flanks when they feel the kittens moving and others roll about on the ground almost as if coming into season.

As the queen nears her time she will be less active and spend more time lying around and indulging in long grooming sessions. She should still be allowed to exercise but try to discourage her from jumping off heights in the later stages of pregnancy. Owing to her altered shape and weight she is liable to make a clumsy landing which could induce a premature birth.

If she is at all inclined to be constipated she should have a large teaspoonful of salad oil or liquid paraffin twice weekly for the last two weeks but in any case she should have a dose just before the kittens are due: hard faeces can very easily obstruct the pelvic cavity, reducing the size of the passage through which the kitten must pass. *Never* give castor oil.

At the end of the eighth week, clip the fur round the mammary glands, the purpose of this being to enable the kittens to reach the teats more easily. Otherwise their tiny claws tend to become caught in the long fine fur. Wash the glands with warm water and mild soap, rinse well and dry. The teats may be massaged with a little olive oil to soften them and remove any oil or wax which may have accumulated there. The washing and oiling may be repeated just before kittening. The fur around the anus and vulva, down the back of the thighs and under the tail should also be clipped because it becomes soiled during parturition. An inexperienced queen may then be too busy cleaning herself to attend to the newly born kitten.

SIGNS OF APPROACHING KITTENING

For a few days before the kittens are due the queen will be restless and no doubt there will be several false alarms before the birth actually takes place. Of course there are always exceptions: some queens produce their kittens with no previous warning and the owner is lucky enough to look in the box and find one or more kittens already present.

If the queen is a maiden, the breeder can have no idea how she will behave but at subsequent litters she is more than likely to repeat her behaviour pattern. I have found it very helpful to make a case history of each kittening so that when the next litter is due I can refer to it and find if and how the queen is deviating from her normal pattern. I note the duration and type of her pre-kittening behaviour until the onset of labour; the quality, frequency and duration of her contractions; the intervals between kittens; the birth position of each kitten; and the time of expulsion of the placenta. I make this case history as detailed as possible for several reasons. It can be a rough guide for future kittening behaviour—it is really not possible to trust to memory for such things. By reading over the history of previous kittenings I find a record of many things I have forgotten and which at the time I was sure I would remember.

The history is helpful also to the veterinary surgeon who may be called upon to know if the queen is usually slow at the job (of course each case must be decided on its own merits but previous behaviour must be taken into account when deciding if intervention is necessary). Writing the case history also occupies my mind and helps to prevent me getting impatient while observing the queen!

## Kittening

The queen will probably like to have the owner, or someone she knows well, at hand while she is in labour. This does not mean that you should be constantly poking about in her box and disturbing her. To be around and speak to her frequently is enough. Sometimes a maiden queen will leap out of the box, run round the room, or even squat in her sanitary tray when she first feels labour pains. She should be put back in her box, calmed and if necessary held in place, while you gently stroke her back and talk to her in a soothing voice until the kitten is produced. Otherwise she may transform some of the energy required for the birth into the energy expended rushing madly about until she is too exhausted to expel the kitten. After the first kitten has arrived she will know what to expect and will be less likely to panic.

HAVE READY

Pieces of clean, soft towelling (old towels cut up into handy sizes); warm water; mild disinfectant; soap and hand towel; a box or basket containing a hot-water bottle securely wrapped in a blanket or towel—this is to put the kittens in should it be necessary; a firm table covered with a clean thick blanket either near a window or under good artificial light—in case veterinary attention is required. Valuable time may be wasted assembling these things should a crisis occur and while veterinary surgeons are prepared to work under difficulties—grovelling about on the floor in the half light if necessary—it is only fair to both them and the queen to have conditions as near perfect as possible.

COMFORT

As well as preparing for the queen's comfort, I like to prepare for my own. I make sure I have a comfortable chair, reading matter—especially those things which I feel I ought to have read and have not—letter-writing materials, mending, knitting and, most important, facilities for making tea or coffee.

The temperature of the room where kittening takes place is of the utmost importance and should not be less than 70°F. The source of heat should not be near the queen or she will become overheated and start panting. If this occurs, reduce the temperature until she is comfortable. The danger of the room temperature being too low is that newly born kittens chill easily and quickly suffer from hypothermia (reduction in body temperature), possibly leading to death. This is even more likely to happen when two kittens are born in quick succession and the mother is unable to lick them both dry in time.

### WHAT TO EXPECT AT THE PERFECT KITTENING

Twenty-four hours before the kittens are born the queen will give warning of the event by becoming restless and paying frequent visits to the kittening box. She may also refuse food for 12 hours or so before the birth. When she feels the birth is imminent she will go in the box, lie down and groom herself thoroughly. Most queens purr on a low crooning note during this period. Quite soon the second stage begins and the labour pains can be seen by contractions of the abdominal muscles and straining movements of the whole hindquarters. These contractions become stronger and more frequent as the kitten passes down the birth canal, reaching a peak when the kitten's head enters the pelvic cavity. Most queens lie on their sides during labour but some will squat, as if trying to expel hard faeces. Some bloodstained fluid is usually expelled first, then a greenish-black bubble appears at the vulva. This is followed by the kitten's head and finally the whole kitten plops out, accompanied by a quantity of blackish green fluid. It may, or may not, still be enclosed in the foetal membranes. If it is, the queen will immediately free the kitten from the membranes so that it can breath and will chew through the cord connecting the kitten to the membranes about 2 inches from the umbilicus. She may or may not eat the placenta. If not, you must remove and dispose of it. If the kitten has emerged from the placenta during its passage down the birth canal, it will still be attached to it by the umbilical cord and the placenta will follow the birth of the kitten almost immediately.

The queen will now spend about half an hour cleaning up the kitten and herself. In some cases the kitten will start to suck but usually this is delayed until all the kittens are born. After this interval for cleaning and a short rest, the whole process will be repeated until the entire litter is born. Within about 3 hours (depending on the number of kittens) the whole business will be over, the kittens cleaned up and dried, all busily sucking and the mother having a snooze.

This is the ideal; do not expect it to happen this way. There are many deviations which need give rise to no anxiety.

DO NOT WORRY IF:

1. The kitten is born hind feet first—almost as many are born this way as head first. It will probably take longer to be born and require greater effort on the part of the queen—the kitten is swimming against the tide, as it were.

2. The queen has a long rest in between kittens—anything up to 2–3 hours, provided she is not having labour pains during this period.

3. The newly born kitten does not start sucking immediately. Just see that it does not get cold and wet while the queen is attending to succeeding kittens. If the queen does not object, the kittens can be removed and kept warm in a blanket on a hot-water bottle until all are born. The quantity of fluid accompanying labour varies enormously and the first-born kittens may become soaked and cold by the fluid from succeeding births.

4. The queen does not appear to have any milk at first. Quite often the milk does not start to flow until all the kittens are born.

TAKE ACTION IF:

1. The queen has *strong* labour pains for two hours and no kitten appears. Contact your veterinary surgeon.

2. The queen has feeble and infrequent contractions which are not increasing in intensity. Stroking her back firmly from withers to tail will sometimes help to stimulate the contractions.

3. Part of the kitten is obtruding from the vulva—the head or the hindlegs, for example—and the queen is unable to expel the whole foetus. Grasp the protruding part in a piece of clean towelling. When the queen strains pull gently but firmly in a backward and slightly downward direction. When the labour pain passes off try to keep hold of the kitten but do *not* pull until the queen strains again. If you are not successful, call your veterinary surgeon immediately.

4. The queen does not free the kitten's head from the foetal membranes within a minute of birth. A maiden queen may not realize quickly enough what she is supposed to do. First try to encourage her to do what is necessary by holding the kitten's head to her mouth. She may be licking herself instead of the kitten, so try to bring the kitten in contact with her tongue. If this fails you must free the kitten's head by tearing the membranes so that it can breathe, then allow the queen to remove the membranes from its body. Supposing she does not chew through the cord within a reasonable time, grasp it very firmly between the finger and thumb of your left hand (first having washed your hands thoroughly). With the other finger and thumb tear the cord apart, making quite sure there is no tension on the cord between the kitten and your left hand. I find that by this method there is less risk of haemorrhage than by cutting the cord with scissors.

FACTORS CAUSING DYSTOKIA (difficulty during parturition)

*The dam*

The shape of the queen's pelvis is of some consequence. It may be too narrow and in extreme cases the kitten's head may be too broad to be able to pass through it. This fault is rare in longhairs and is more likely to be seen in breeds such as Siamese, which have slim narrow bodies.

On the other hand the pelvic cavity may be too flattened dorso-ventrally. This means that the brim of the pelvis is too high, especially if there is a large litter as their sheer weight drags the abdomen down and the kittens have what amounts to an uphill crawl to the outside world. With this pelvic formation the kittening is likely to be a prolonged and exhausting one.

Queens with either of these faults should not be bred from again.

The pelvis may have become malformed due to fracture in an accident or by a fall when the queen was a kitten. If the malformation is of sufficient severity to cause difficulty in parturition the cat should be spayed.

The presence of even a small quantity of hard faeces in the rectum may so occlude the pelvic cavity that the kitten is unable to pass through it. In this case an enema will clear the obstruction but probably not in time to save the first kitten, who will have been too long in transit before the cause of the trouble has been discovered. This is certainly an unnecessary hazard and one easily avoided by the routine administration of a laxative to the queen.

### Uterine inertia

This means that the muscles of the uterus are slow to act and therefore labour contractions are feeble and may be insufficient to expel the kitten. If the inertia is complete, contractions are totally absent. Inertia is fairly common in longhairs, especially in queens confined to a cattery who have had insufficient exercise during pregnancy and whose muscles therefore lack tone. A hereditary factor may also be involved, because the condition is sometimes seen to run in families. Obviously such a line should be discontinued.

A queen who has a prolonged labour is not, however, necessarily suffering from inertia. Some are naturally slow and may have a long rest, even some hours, between kittens. Inertia applies rather to the quality of the uterine contractions. These may be stimulated by injection of oxytocin. If finally all efforts to overcome the inertia fail, caesarian section must be performed.

### The kitten

Foetal monstrosities are fortunately rarely seen in felines. Occasionally a case of hydrocephalus (fluid in the brain cavity) may cause difficulty on account of the enlargement of the head.

Actual size must be taken into account for a kitten can impede its own birth simply by being too large. This is quite

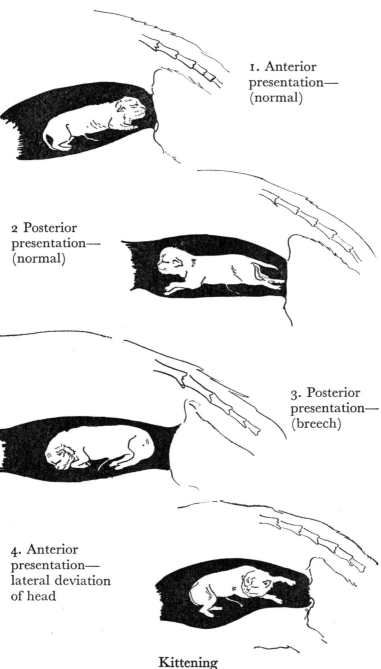

1. Anterior presentation— (normal)

2 Posterior presentation— (normal)

3. Posterior presentation— (breech)

4. Anterior presentation— lateral deviation of head

Kittening

often seen in longhairs when the litters are small and the kittens large.

The most common cause of dystokia on the part of the kitten is its abnormal presentation. The normal birth position is head first (see Fig. 1). In this case the position of the forelimbs does not seem to matter greatly in cats, who have pliable and comparatively short leg bones as compared to the foal or calf whose legs are long, with the bones sufficiently calcified to enable it to stand immediately after birth. Almost as often the tail and hind limbs are presented and this can really be regarded as normal, although the birth will be slower, as the kitten's movements do not help (see Fig. 2). This, contrary to many people's belief, is not a breech birth. The true breech birth is when only the tail and buttocks are presented, while the hindlegs point towards the kitten's head (see Fig. 3).

When coming head first, the kitten's neck may become twisted, so that the back of the head or the side of the neck (see Fig. 4) is presented. This delivery will require digital manipulation to correct it and unless you are very experienced should be left to your veterinary surgeon. In some cases caesarian section will be necessary.

Sometimes a kitten from each horn of the uterus will start to be born and by arriving simultaneously at the cervix will cause a complete hold up. Caesarian section is usually necessary.

A kitten may miss the entrance to the birth canal and lie transversely with its head in one horn and hindquarters in the other. Again Caesarian section is required.

## ABORTION

This is quite common in cats and often occurs about the third week of pregnancy, when the cat will be seen to have a bloody discharge. She will probably call again very soon. Occurring at this stage, the abortion may be due to a uterine infection and the cat will require treatment before being mated again. Or hormonal secretion may be deficient. Abortion also occurs at the 7th–8th week, from similar causes, or at this stage there could be an external cause such as an emotional upset or a fall.

At whatever stage an abortion occurs it is advisable to have a veterinary investigation into possible causes before sending the queen to stud again.

FALSE PREGNANCY

It may be that after all the signs of being in kitten—pink teats, enlarged abdomen, making of nests and even milk production—the kittening date will come and go and, instead of kittens arriving, the queen's body will gradually return to normal and she may well begin to call again.

This can have been a true psuedo-cyesis when no ova were fertilized but the hormone of pregnancy was secreted, or possibly the ova were fertilized and implantation took place only for the foetuses to become resorbed at some stage in their development. It is advisable to consult your veterinary surgeon before mating her again.

## The kittens

AFTER CARE

When the kittens have all been born, cleaned up and the queen shows signs of settling down, tidy the bed, removing any badly soiled paper. If the queen resents this being done, leave it till later. Offer her a warm milky drink, have a quick look at the kittens to see that all appear to be well, then leave the family in peace so that the queen can have a good rest and sleep if she wants.

Keep the room temperature at 70°F for the present, gradually reducing it as the kittens grow and become active. Do not allow any strangers to visit the queen until you are sure she is happy to have them. It is natural to want to show the kittens to friends and neighbours but you will have to be guided by your cat's feelings in the matter. Some queens will not mind at all and are proud to show off their kittens; others will become disturbed and may desert the kittens or drag them to another bed. If there are young children in the house, do not let them handle the newly born kittens; they are quite incapable of knowing when they are squeezing too hard and also may drop the kittens accidentally. By all means let the children look when the queen is happy for them to do so but never leave children alone with kittens (or any other young animals for that matter) until you are quite certain the children are old enough to treat them properly—a great many kittens are injured by being treated as toys by children. This not only causes pain to the kitten but in most cases causes distress to the child as well.

When the queen has had a rest offer her some food and drinking water should of course always be available to her. Have her sanitary tray within easy reach of her bed. To begin with some queens can hardly bear to leave their kittens for long enough to go to the tray. If she has not relieved herself within 24 hours then you should place her on the tray and hope she will use it. Do not touch the kittens while the queen is away from them. Later on when the kittens are bigger she won't mind.

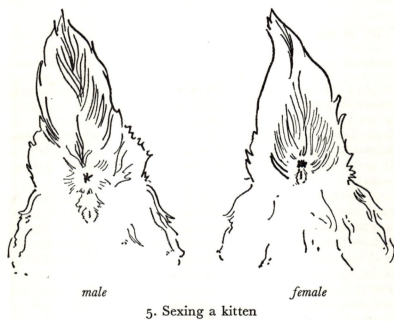

*male*                    *female*

5. Sexing a kitten

See that the kittens are all sucking and lying close to their mother. If one kitten is lying apart from the rest, put it back with the others and then if you again see it pushed to one side there is no doubt that something is wrong. Examine it for any abnormality, such as a cleft palate and take it away from the mother, keeping it warm until you can get veterinary help.

The queen may or may not have a slight bloody discharge for a day or two after kittening. If this is copious, or thick and containing pus, she will require treatment. Sometimes it may be caused by a retained placenta or an infection of the uterus. In this case she will have a rise of temperature and be off colour. A slight rise of body temperature for 48 hours after the kittens are born is quite usual. Perhaps this is nature's way of keeping the kittens warm enough. No action need be taken if the queen is bright and eating well.

You will want to sex the kittens and have a good look at them and this can be done as soon as the queen is not worried by your handling of them. Just examine one kitten at a time and don't take it out of her sight—she will be happier if she sees what you are doing.*

While the kittens are very small, inspect the queen's mammary glands daily. The two posterior glands often prove difficult for tiny kittens to suckle and if they are swollen and hard apply hot fomentations and milk them until the milk is flowing freely. Mastitis can develop if the glands are not emptied and this can lead to the formation of a breast abscess. It does not matter if some of the glands are not used by the kittens, provided they are not producing milk. This often happens when there are only two or three kittens.

If the mother is able and willing to look after the kittens, although she cannot feed them owing to a failure in her milk supply, you may have to hand-feed one or more kittens. A kitten's feeding bottle can be obtained from most pet shops or, in case of emergency, use an eye dropper with one inch of bicycle-valve tubing on the open end. Kittens quickly learn to suck on the rubber tubing. Make up dried milk as used for babies to double strength and add a little glucose, or use cow's milk mixed with egg yolk. Dr Patricia Scott advises one part beaten egg yolk to four parts of cow's milk. In the beginning the

---

* Holding the kitten on the palm of one hand with its tail towards you, with the finger and thumb of the other hand raise the tail gently. Male. Locate the anus at the root of the tail. Below this it is usually possible to see two tiny bumps side by side where the testicles will be later on. Below that again and equidistant is a small round slightly raised orifice—the sheath of the penis. Female. Locate the anus, and almost immediately below it is a slit, the vulva, which is the entrance to the vagina. This orifice is much closer to the anus than is that of the male.

H

kittens will need feeding every two hours day and night, so by the time you have prepared the feeds, fed them and had some food and sleep yourself there will be no time for anything else. After the first few days you can probably reduce the night feeds to three-hourly intervals, provided the kittens are thriving and can adapt to a longer interval.

It sometimes happens that a maiden queen will have nothing to do with the kittens, or she may be too unwell to look after them, or just occasionally a queen will die during kittening. When possible transfer one or all of the kittens to a feline foster-mother, because cat's milk is always better for kittens than cow's, goat's or bitch's milk. A bitch can sometimes be coaxed to look after young kittens but you should hand-feed the kittens because canine milk is not rich enough in protein. To find a foster cat, ask all the cat breeders you know, local veterinary surgeons and the cat welfare societies. Often these people will know of a cat who has only one or two kittens of her own and a plentiful milk supply. Your kittens need not necessarily all go to one foster.

Supposing a foster cat is not available, you must then look after them yourself like a mother. This means keeping them warm on a cosy blanket either under an infra-red lamp or on a hot-water bottle, which must be refilled frequently, and attending to their toilet. As soon as you have fed a kitten, wipe its face clean with damp cotton wool then turn to its other end and stroke gently under its tail, again with damp cotton wool. This encourages it to urinate and defecate, a stimulus normally supplied by the mother's tongue. Once daily, wipe the kitten all over with damp cotton wool under a source of warmth and dry gently with a piece of towelling.

For the first three weeks or so, the kittens will need very little attention from you. When their eyes open at around ten days see that they are opening properly. If the lids stick together, bathe them gently and smear on a little vaseline. Should there be any discharge of pus, antibiotic drops or ointment will be required. Be on the look out generally for any signs of ill health.

While she is feeding the kittens, the mother cat needs her normal amount of foods plus a ration to enable her to produce plenty of good rich milk for the kittens. Extra fluid can be given in the form of evaporated or dried milk, or some cow's milk if she can digest it. Or she might like gravy or beef essence. If she is not one who likes fluids, make her feeds more sloppy than normal. Her food must contain plenty of protein and a supplement of cod-liver oil or Adexolin drops and also calcium and phosphorus in the correct proportion. Mineral additives can be bought in pet shops or at some chemists.

The quantity of food given will depend on the cat herself and the number of kittens she is nursing. As long as her digestive system is not upset, give her as much as she will take.

Do not forget that occasionally a queen will come in season again quite soon after the kittens are born, although most cats won't until after weaning, so only let her out in the garden under supervision.

WEANING AND FEEDING

At about four weeks of age you can start weaning the kittens and this should be a very gradual process, to allow the kitten's digestive system plenty of time to adapt itself and for the mother's milk supply to decrease. I use double-strength dried milk for babies, plus a little glucose, and start by giving one teaspoonful once daily. I warm it to blood heat and offer it to the kitten in a teaspoon, just touching the kitten's lips with the liquid. Feed the kittens when they have just wakened up—before they have had time to suck—so that they are hungry. You will find some kittens much quicker than others at learning to lap. When the kittens are taking the milk well, I thicken it with some baby cereal and then as soon as their baby teeth have come through I give them minced rabbit or fish. I find that longhair kittens are not ready to digest raw meat until about eight weeks old, at which point I give them scraped cow beef. Siamese and shorthair kittens seem to be able to cope with meat at a much earlier age.

So far as food is concerned the kittens should be entirely independent of their mothers by eight weeks old and at this age they will need five feeds per day. I usually give three protein feeds and two milky and vary the feeds as much as possible, giving a meaty feed last thing to sustain the kittens during the night. The actual food is the same as for adult cats but minced or mashed. I do not use any tinned food until the kittens are at least three months old and then only if fresh food is not available.

The number of feeds per day is reduced until at six months the kitten is having three solid feeds, plus a milky feed, and at nine months onwards two feeds, plus milk if this does not upset it.

As the kittens are weaned they will begin to take less and less from their mother and her extra rations can be decreased. She will leave the kittens for longer and longer periods but she should still be allowed to be with them as much as she wants because it is her job to discipline and train them and to play with them. The kittens learn by copying their mother and she is not slow to growl at or slap them when they are doing wrong or getting too obstreperous.

When the kittens are big enough to climb out of the box, put a sanitary tray near by. It is amazing how quickly they learn to use it. The sides of the tray must be low so that the kittens can easily get in and out—an old roasting tin will do very well. Now the kittens should be confined in a large pen, firstly for their own safety—they are so easily trodden on or squashed in a doorway at this age—and secondly so that they do not stray too far from their lavatory. If they get too far away, they do not have time to get back to the tray and squat in any corner.

IMMUNIZATION

The only disease in cats against which there is an effective vaccine is feline infectious enteritis. From time to time vaccines against the viral respiratory diseases have been produced but, owing to the numbers and variations of viruses involved, these have not always been entirely satisfactory.

There is no doubt whatsoever that the immunization of kittens against FIE has reduced its incidence until it is rare nowadays to hear of an authenticated case. By 'authenticated' I mean a case in which the causal organism has been isolated. Enteritis in cats from various causes is still common, notably bacteria of the Salmonella group and as they both give rise to similar symptoms the two diseases may be confused.

Unless you are a conscientious objector to vaccination it is advisable to have all your kittens inoculated. Your veterinary surgeon will advise you about the type of vaccine to be used and also at what age it should be carried out. This will depend on the health and sturdiness of your kittens, local conditions etc. Kittens can be inoculated at a few weeks old but at this age the immunity only lasts a short time and a second inoculation is necessary after 12 weeks of age.

The cost of the inoculation will of course add to the expense of kitten-rearing but it is usual to add this to the price of the kitten. I have yet to meet a serious buyer who is put off by the added cost. They are usually only too pleased that it has been done.

Nowadays there can be very few first-rate boarding catteries who accept unimmunized cats and I would not myself board my cats at any place which did.

### PEDIGREES, REGISTRATIONS, TRANSFERS AND PREFIXES

*Pedigrees*

The dictionary defines the word 'pedigree' as 'a list or table of descent and relationship'. This is exactly what appears on a pedigree form. It lists the cat's sire and dam, the grandparents, the great grandparents and great-great-grandparents, giving the names and the breed numbers.

If earlier generations are required, it is possible to pay a fee to the registrar of the Governing Council of the Cat Fancy to search as far back as is required, the charge depending on the number of ancestors involved. A certified pedigree is then issued. This is frequently asked for by overseas buyers, when importing stock into their country from Britain. It is then usually referred to as an export pedigree certificate and assures the buyer that the breeding is as stated on the pedigree.

If a male kitten or male adult is being sent overseas, a certificate of entirety must be sent. This is issued by a veterinary surgeon, on payment of a fee, and is proof, as far as can be ascertained by an examination, that the male is fully developed, that is has both testicles and should be capable of siring kittens.

*Registration*

No pedigree cat or kitten can be exhibited unless it has been previously registered with the Governing Council of the Cat Fancy.

To register a kitten, an application form has to be filled in giving the cat's name, details of parentage and date of birth. This should be sent with the correct fee to the appropriate registrar. On acceptance a certificate will be issued bearing the cat's official registered number and the other details; the number and name are for life and cannot be changed in any detail.

## Prefixes

If you intend to go in for breeding seriously it is advisable to apply for a prefix. This is a distinguishing name used before each registered kitten's individual name and may be used by the owner alone. Using a prefix solves not only the problem of choosing names that have not already been used, but, if you are exhibiting and winning at the shows, your cattery name will soon become well known, which is a good advertisement. It is necessary to be a member of an affiliated cat club before one is permitted to own a prefix. On payment of the fee, and after approval by the Governing Council, the prefix is registered and becomes the owner's for life.

## Transfer

Once a registered kitten has been sold it should be transferred officially to the new owner. It is not always realized that even if the new owner has the registration form and pedigree from the breeder, until the kitten has been transferred to him, it cannot be shown in his name. The application for transfer signed by both parties, together with the correct fee, should be sent to the Governing Council as soon as possible after purchase. On acceptance, a transfer form will be sent to the new owner.

If entering for a show the transfer should have been effected at least three weeks beforehand, otherwise it may mean disqualification, with loss of entry fees and any possible winnings.

## Affix

In Britain an affix, that is a name after the kitten's own name, is not now allowed. Only a few of those granted many years ago are still being used and these will die out.

### SELLING

Well-known breeders whose cats do a lot of winning at shows usually have little difficulty in selling kittens, in fact they often have a list of people waiting to buy a kitten of their breeding. For the novice breeder the selling of kittens is a different matter. Sometimes the stud owner will be able to help if she has more enquiries for kittens than she can satisfy from her own stock. Very often friends who have seen and admired your queen will want to have one of her kittens. At one time I had an unusual source of enquiries—my garden was overlooked by travellers on the top deck of double-decker buses and I had several people wanting to buy kittens through having seen the cats in the garden. One of the very best homes that my kittens went to was by this channel.

If you think your kittens are up to show standard, an advertisement in *Fur and Feather* will bring them to the notice of other breeders and potential cat fanciers. You can also exhibit them when they are old enough and try to sell them at the show but in this case do make searching enquiries about the buyer, in case it should be a dealer buying them for resale. You would have no idea then of what kind of home your kittens were going to. Be wary of anyone who wants to buy several kittens at once.

You can also advertise in local or national newspapers, although the latter is fairly expensive.

By whatever method you dispose of kittens, do please try to make sure they are going to suitable homes. Whenever possible, take the kitten to its new home and see it settled in.

For your part, never sell a kitten that is in less than perfect health. The stress of changing homes is certain to aggravate any slight illness, such as an upset tummy, and neither the kitten nor the buyer will be happy if it is ill immediately after it arrives.

The kitten should have been de-wormed at about 5–6 weeks old, under veterinary supervision, and, if practicable, should be inoculated against feline infectious enteritis before leaving home. Before you are to hand over the kitten, get ready a copy of its pedigree, its registration certificate, inoculation certificate and a transfer form to be filled in when the sale is complete. I am constantly getting complaints from people who have bought a kitten (or a puppy for that matter) and have had immense difficulty in getting the relevant papers from the breeder. In almost all cases this is due to laziness, not knavery, but it is very tiresome for the buyer.

## EXPORT

Nearly all countries differ slightly in their import regulations and these may be changed from time to time, so if you are exporting a cat or kitten it is essential to get in touch with the Ministry of Agriculture, Fisheries and Food, Tolworth, Surbiton, Surrey—well in advance of the date of export—to find out what is required. Some countries require cats to be vaccinated against rabies before leaving this country. At present these include Germany, New Zealand and Switzerland. Application must be made to the Ministry six weeks before the date of export and the veterinary surgeon who administers the vaccine must have written proof from the owner that the animal is being exported. This is because rabies vaccination is not normally permitted in this country.

Most countries want a health certificate from a veterinary surgeon and this generally has to be one who holds an appointment as a local veterinary inspector of the Ministry.

Cats may only be sent to New Zealand by sea; they can, however, now be sent to Australia by sea—but arrangements must be made well ahead. In Australia the cat will usually have to go into quarantine for 120 days, although this may be reduced to 60 days on certain conditions being fulfilled.

The United States and Canada do not at present require any certificates but the shipping company may want a health certificate signed by a veterinary surgeon.

Movement of cats is unrestricted between Great Britain, Northern Ireland, Republic of Ireland, Isle of Man and the Channel Islands.

A pedigree cat will also need an export pedigree certificate, obtainable from the registrar of the GCCF in order to be registered in its new country. In the case of a male cat, a veterinary certificate stating that the cat is entire (both testicles in the normal position in the scrotum) must be sent to the registrar when applying for the export pedigree.

## IMPORT AND QUARANTINE

All cats entering the UK from other countries must, without exception, spend six months in a quarantine cattery approved by the Ministry of Agriculture, Fisheries and Food before being allowed to live with the owner. Before importing a cat, you should get the addresses of these catteries from the Ministry and choose one reasonably near your home as you will probably be allowed to visit the cat. Each cattery is registered in the name of a veterinary surgeon, who inspects the cats daily.

On arrival in this country, the cat must be met at the dock or airport and transported to the cattery by an approved carrier, not by the owner.

Importing a cat is not a thing to be embarked on lightly. It will be fairly expensive and six months is a long time for a cat to spend in a cattery, away from its owners.

# Chapter five

# Grooming

The basic equipment needed to groom and clean a longhaired cat is:

*Hairbrush*

Bristle tufts are better for the coat than nylon. I use a brush with a narrow rectangular-shaped head and fairly long bristles, because I find it easier to get to the roots of the hair with that rather than the usual broad oval shape.

*Steel combs*

For the tail and for preliminary body combing use a comb with fairly widely spaced teeth. For thorough combing use a comb with medium spacing. For the short hair on the head and face use a fine-tooth comb, which can also be used on the body to search for fleas and their excreta.

*Cotton wool and cotton-wool buds*

For cleaning eyes and ears.

*Scissors*

For cutting any tangles or soiled hair. Blunt points are essential because if the cat moves suddenly you may give it a nasty jab with pointed scissors. The size and shape of the scissors is a matter of personal choice.

*Bay rum*

For use on glossy coats such as black. A proprietary lotion, or *eau-de-Cologne* can be substituted.

*Talcum powder*

The use of powder helps to keep the coat clean and free from tangles and it is an essential part of show preparation for many light-coated breeds.

*Nail clippers*

To trim the sharp points of the nails as necessary. Cats can sharpen their nails only too well but, especially as they grow older, do not always wear them down sufficiently. If you feel apprehensive about cutting nails yourself, your veterinary surgeon will do the job for you.

Although there are differences in methods of grooming in varieties of longhaired cats the reason is the same for all: to remove all dead hair from the coat. If this is not done the coat becomes tangled, which is not only uncomfortable for the cat but means that the coat loses its insulating properties because matted hair cannot trap a layer of air to effect insulation. A longhaired cat with a really thick coat is quite unable to remove all the dead hair itself without swallowing a considerable quantity and this will lead to the formation of furball in the stomach or intestine.

Another reason for regular grooming is that the cat appears to its best advantage. Of course, however much a coat is groomed, if the cat itself is not in good condition it will never look its very best. If you intend to show your cat then grooming becomes more important still. A badly groomed cat stands little chance on the show bench. If groomed regularly, most cats grow to love it and will become quite impatient when waiting their turn on the grooming table. It is a good opportunity for cat and owner to make physical contact and establish a bond between them, especially for those cats who dislike being picked up or handled at any other time.

An important reason for regular grooming is that it enables the owner to discover anything wrong with the cat such as fleas, abscesses, wounds, skin diseases etc. before they get a chance to become established or complications set in.

It is really never too young to start grooming. Even young kittens can be brushed gently with a soft hairbrush—a baby's brush is just the thing. If you mean to show your cat or kitten and you are a novice, ask the breeder to show you how it should be done for that particular breed.

Some people like to have the cat on their lap for grooming, others prefer to have it standing on a table. The best method is the one that suits you and your cat. It is a great help if the cat will lie on its back, either on your lap or on the table, for its tummy to be groomed but some will not tolerate this. In such a case it is usually possible to reach all areas by lifting one leg at a time.

In all longhair breeds the fur in front of the shoulders should be brushed forward to train it to stand out as a frame for the cat's head. In most of the breeds the body hair wants to stand out and should be brushed outward and the tail hair brushed out but in the case of breeds with markings such as the tabbies, the fur must be arranged to show off the markings. The undercoat can be fluffed out but a comb should then be used to put the coat in place and show up the stripes.

Everyone has their own methods and routine for grooming; some start by brushing the coat out, others use the comb first—so long as the end result is what you want it doesn't matter how you achieve it. What does matter is that the coat should be brushed and combed right to the roots. With a thick longhair coat it is only too easy to slide over tangled hair and just brush out the top layer. So be sure to part the coat with one hand while grooming with the other and you can then see that you are reaching down to the skin.

Any tangled hair should be gently teased apart by hand and also by combing and brushing. If the fur is too felted, then the mats must be carefully cut off taking great care not to cut the cat's skin. Longhaired cats have very thin skin and if you pull on the tangle to reach it for cutting, then remember a fold of skin will come too. If for any reason you have been unable to cope with grooming the cat and the coat is completely tangled and knotted, your veterinary surgeon can give the cat a general anaesthetic and get rid of the mats either by combing or cutting or a combination of both. If you do have to cut any fur, the cat should not be exhibited until the coat has grown again. The show rules state that a cat whose coat has been wrongly prepared for show, for example by cutting or dying, should be disqualified.

As well as attending to the cat's coat, see that its eyes and ears are clean and once or twice weekly examine teeth and nails. Most longhair cats gather a little discharge at the inner corner of the eye and this should be gently wiped away with a piece of damp cotton wool. Next look inside the ears and if they appear clean do nothing; please don't go poking around inside the ears as a matter of routine. If there is any trouble in the ear canal the cat will soon let you know by shaking its head or scratching the ear with a hind foot. The lining of the ear is very delicate and great discomfort and even pain is often caused to cats by well-meaning owners using strong or unsuitable lotions and powders. Some cats produce a greasy material on the inner surface of the ear flap or at the top of the ear canal and this can be removed by using a cotton-wool bud, either dry or damp. A dark reddish-brown discharge in the ear usually indicates the presence of ear mites, which should be treated under veterinary supervision. It is not necessary to dispose only of the mites, the inflammation they cause and any secondary infections must be dealt with too. There is no single treatment for ear-mite infection: what may suit one case will not necessarily work on the next.

Check the mouth and teeth once a week, or more often if necessary, especially in kittens and aged cats. In kittens keep a look out for mouth ulcers, inflamed gums and teething troubles. Occasionally kittens fail to shed their baby or milk teeth and these may have to be extracted if they are causing the second teeth to erupt in the wrong place. In older cats look for formation of tartar on the teeth. This should be removed, otherwise bacteria invade the gums and the teeth become loose and drop out or have to be extracted.

It is not always necessary to look at cats' nails to be only too painfully aware that they are too long but old cats sometimes suffer from ingrowing nails so check them at least once weekly, especially the dew claws on the front legs—because they are not worn down at all these are the ones most likely to grow in a circle.

GROOMING FOR A SHOW

Presentation makes an enormous difference to an exhibit. If two cats are of much the same standard for type and colour then the one with the well-cared-for coat will naturally always have an advantage over the one with dirty paws, stained trousers and a rough coat. Even the not-so-good exhibit can always gain points for coat and condition so why not give your cat every chance by making sure it is as well prepared as possible.

Factors which can spoil a coat's appearance are: too much sunshine on a black coat will give it a rusty appearance; some types of cat litter can stain the cat's feet (I once had chinchillas with pink feet when I tried a new type of litter); the mother cat by excessive licking may make the tips of her kitten's coat brown.

The final preparations will vary according to breed and of course every exhibitor has his or her own method and ideas on how to do things.

Speaking generally, breeds such as the blues, creams and blue-creams are prepared by lavish use of talcum powder. This is sprinkled into the coat, then thoroughly brushed out again. It keeps the coat clean and separates the individual hairs so that the coat stands out well. Some cats have a greasy patch on the tail and this can be dealt with either by cleansing with a little surgical spirit or else by shampooing the tail. This is most easily done by sitting the cat on the draining board and dipping the tail in a bucket of water in the sink. Use soap or a human-hair shampoo and not detergent and rinse several times. Dry well and comb while drying to fluff out the hair. The final powdering should be done two days before the show so that on the last day the powder can be thoroughly brushed out. Any powder left in the coat may cause the cat to be disqualified and powdering causes some cats to have weepy eyes temporarily— this might mean being turned down at the vetting-in.

Breeds with glossy coats, such as blacks and torties, should not be powdered. Some breeders use bran sprinkled into the roots before being brushed out again to clean the coat. To make the coat shine, *eau-de-Cologne*, bay rum or proprietary lotions can be applied and a final polish given with a silk handkerchief.

In place of talcum powder, in the breeds that have dark as well as light hair, such as tabbies and colour-points, Fuller's earth can be used. This should be natural, not refined.

Chinchillas and white cats almost always include a bath in their show preparation, especially those who live a free outdoor life. The bath should take place several days before the show so that the coat has time to regain its natural 'bounce' and this should be assisted by final powdering as for the blues etc.

*All* preparations for the bath should be made in advance: you cannot leave a soaking-wet cat sitting on a table while you run upstairs to fetch a towel. No doubt you will evolve your own order for giving it a bath and how you do it will depend to a large extent on the help you have available. The late Mrs Emilie Polden, whose cats were always perfectly prepared, had a marvellous single-handed method consisting of a line of plastic bowls of lukewarm water, ending up with a bucket of water for the final dunking. I have always been lucky enough to have helpers available, and so I get my cats accustomed to sitting on the draining board, restrained by a helper, while I wet the coat with a spray. Mostly the cats prefer the spray to being immersed in water. If you do put the cat in water in the sink, then put a rubber mat or an old towel on the bottom because cats hate to feel their feet slipping.

Before the bath I assemble:

*Cotton wool*—to plug the ears and prevent water getting in.
*Shampoos*—Johnson's Baby Shampoo for the face and head and any normal hair shampoo for the rest of the body.
*Old cups*—for mixing the shampoos with some water. They penetrate the coat better if diluted.
*Towels*—warm and plenty of them.
*Large cat basket*—to put the cat in, on a warm towel.
*Hair-dryer and combs*—some cats will allow a hair-dryer to be used.

Having shampooed and rinsed the cat well, I dry it as much as possible with thick warm towels (not forgetting to remove the cotton wool from the ears). Then if the cat agrees, a helper holds it while I blow the hair with the drier, combing it at the same time and trying to arrange the fur as I want it to go. If the cat dislikes the hair-drier, I have it comfortably near a source of heat and comb it frequently, fluffing up the hair to make the coat stand out.

After the cat has been bathed it simply must be confined to one clean room until the show—or all your good work will be in vain. The white or chinchilla coat will show up the slightest stain or mark.

Finally, before you set out for the show, check that all is well with the cat—better to have to wash dirty trousers at home rather than at the show. Then all that should be necessary before penning the cat is a final and thorough brushing.

# Chapter six

# Showing

---

Cat shows are the shop windows of the Cat Fancy. They enable breeders to exhibit their stock and by the results to assess the quality; to become well-known for their cats—and also to sell them. Cat shows, too, give pleasure to thousands, for by visiting them they are able to see the elegance and charm of the most beautiful cats and kittens in the country.

The most recent highlight of the British Cat Fancy was the largest cat show in the world organized by the National Cat Club as their centenary show in 1971. Nearly 2,000 cats and kittens entered, with judges officiating from various countries overseas, as well as more than 80 from Britain alone. A letter of congratulation was received from Queen Elizabeth II.

## The show organization in Britain

There are more than 50 cat shows held annually in Britain; the majority have championship status, while the remainder are sanction and exemption shows. Several of the last-named are held in conjunction with local agricultural and county shows.

All these shows come under the jurisdiction of the Governing Council of the Cat Fancy and have to be run strictly in accordance with the rules and regulations set out by them. At one meeting each year, applications for shows are considered by the Council, when the venue, the date and the name of the proposed show manager are all taken into consideration. A list of the shows so approved is issued annually, and may be obtained from the secretary of the Council.

Before any club is given permission to organize a show, it must have applied for, and been granted, affiliation. Prior to this, it should have been in existence for at least three years and have a membership of 100 or more.

At first the club will apply for an exemption show, which is a small one, where prizes are given but no challenge certificates and the classes are not very numerous. After running several such shows successfully, permission may be granted for a sanction show. This is really a rehearsal for a championship show, with the rules and the actual organization required being very similar. Prizes are given but again no challenge certificates. At these shows well-known judges officiate and exhibitors are able to assess the potentialities of their stock before showing at the much bigger championship shows.

Should the way the club has run several sanction shows meet with the approval of the Council, it may grant permission for the running of a much-coveted championship show. This is not as a matter of course, as there are now so many clubs, and as the Council endeavour if possible to space the shows with 14 days between them it is very difficult to fit in all the applications received.

The organization of a show is in the hands of the show manager and her show committee. The running of a show will start many months beforehand, with the booking of the judges who are to officiate, the booking of a suitable hall and the pens and benching. Arrangements must be made regarding the catering for the hall and the supply of tables for the judges' use. A circular letter is sent out to all clubs and many of the fanciers asking for show support, for adverts in the catalogue and for would-be stall-holders to book stands. The clubs usually guarantee classes and offer special prizes for their members only. Fanciers too may guarantee classes for breeds in which they are particularly interested and which they would like divided into male or female. Many, also, offer special prizes.

Guaranteeing a class means that if the monies paid for entering the class by the exhibitors do not cover the cost of the prize money to be paid out for it, the guarantor agrees to pay the difference, so that the club running the show is not the loser.

When the show support is in, there is the complicated task of preparing copy schedule for the printer. The schedule lists the open breed classes, the many miscellaneous classes (for example breeders for cat or kittens bred by the exhibitors) and the classes guaranteed by the various clubs. Judges have to be allocated their classes, with show managers endeavouring to give each judge a fairly equal number of exhibits to handle.

In due course the schedules are sent out in their hundreds to would-be exhibitors, together with the entry forms, and the rules under which the show has to be run. The closing date has to be many weeks before the show day, as it is from the entry forms that the copy for the catalogue is compiled by the show manager. This means many, many hours of hard work, often into the early hours to get such copy to the printer in time. Extra work too will be caused by exhibitors having entered their cats in the wrong classes, which have to be sorted out, or they may have sent in insufficient entry money and so must be written to. A list of exhibitors, their names and addresses and the number allocated to their cats has to be prepared in alphabetical order to go in the end of the catalogue.

Once the catalogue copy has gone to the printer, the hall plan has to be prepared, showing the proposed layout of the pens for the benching firm. The tallies, vetting-in and passing-out cards have to be written out and sent to each exhibitor. Posters have to be sent out for display and advertisements put in the newspapers.

The judging books have also to be written out in triplicate, with all repeats marked. The various small items necessary for the smooth running of the show, such as pencils, pens, drawing-pins must be bought and the flowers ordered for the hall decorations. Last-minute checks must be made to see that there are sufficient towels and bowls and disinfectant for the judges' and veterinary surgeons' use. A check too must be made to make sure that every judge has a steward and that there will be sufficient helpers in the hall to do all the necessary jobs, such as manning the pay box, selling catalogues, serving the judges coffee—and so on.

The show manager will spend the day prior to the show in the hall where the pens will be being erected; stall-holders may be arriving with their stock and various helpers will be putting up the draping around the tabling. She will be there until early evening checking that all the numbers are up before she leaves and that everything is laid out ready for the veterinary surgeon to start the vetting-in in the morning.

However early she gets to the hall in the morning, the first arrivals will be waiting outside ready for the vetting-in, many having driven through the night with their cats. In a very short time the show will be underway.

## Exhibiting

Having bought a kitten and decided that you would like to exhibit, it is important to make sure that the registration formalities have been carried out in good time. Should you not have received your transfer certificate when the entry form is filled in, a note should be put on the form stating that the transfer has been applied for.

It is not necessary to exhibit at shows to breed cats successfully as a hobby; some people dislike the whole idea but the fact remains that it adds considerably to one's prestige and also to their value if your cats and kittens shown do well, winning many prizes. It is as well for the would-be exhibitor to visit at least one show beforehand to get some idea of the routine involved.

Before entering a cat its temperament must be taken into consideration and this depends a great deal on the upbringing. If living in a quiet household, never having been handled by or seen few visitors, it may be very nervous, even frightened, on being put in a small pen to be handled by strangers. If it shows its dislike physically, hitting out at the judges and stewards, it is as well not to show it again.

Most would-be exhibitors belong to a cat club and, if belonging to the one organizing the show, may enter at a reduced rate. Members of the club are sent a schedule and entry forms but, if you are not a member, application should be made to the organizer at least two months before the date of the show enclosing a large stamped, addressed envelope.

To gain experience it is really better to exhibit first at a small local exemption show rather than plunge in at the deep end and enter one of the larger shows, such as that organized by the National Cat Club, where competition is fierce with many hundreds of cats being entered. Remember too that a cat may not be shown twice in 14 days so of course cannot be entered for shows in consecutive weeks.

The schedule contains details of the various classes, gives the names of the judges, particulars of the entry fees, the prize monies and also the many valuable cups and specials offered by the various clubs. Most clubs guarantee classes at each other's shows for their members only.

The rules and regulations should be most carefully studied before filling in the entry form. This requires you to state details of the cat's name, its parentage, date of birth, registration number, name of breeder, the numbers of the chosen classes and your membership of any clubs. The form must be filled in correctly, with details as set out in the registration or transfer form (otherwise disqualification may result), and sent with the entry fees to the show manager, well before the given closing date, usually five to six weeks before the show. If received after the closing date it will doubtless be returned owing to lack of space for late entries.

The choice of classes may seem bewildering to a beginner but the number that may be entered by one cat is restricted to 12, which helps a little. If it is the cat's first show it is as well to enter in only three or four to see how it behaves. From a prestige point of view, the open breed classes are the most important. There are open breed classes for kittens but only cats are eligible for challenge certificates for a win in their class. It is not necessary to be a member of a club running the show to enter—or indeed a member of any club—but the more clubs one belongs to, the more classes there are to enter. If you are a member of the club organizing the show, there is a reduction in the fee for each class entered. Other classes include those for: senior cats (over two years); junior (under two years); cats that have not won more than four first prizes; *débutant(e)s* that have never been exhibited before—and many others.

A kitten is considered to become an adult at nine months and can compete in the open breed class for adults. Neuters cannot compete with full cats but only in classes specifically for them. Their open classes are known as premier classes (see pages 129–30.)

The prize money is small and some clubs do not give prize money in the open class at all but the honour of winning one of the red first-prize cards is much coveted.

Seven to ten days prior to the show each exhibitor should receive a numbered disc and vetting-in and passing-out cards for each of the entries. As this is the first intimation that the entry has been received, many exhibitors enclose a stamped addressed postcard when sending theirs in, which the show manager sends back on receipt.

## The show day

ESSENTIALS TO TAKE TO THE SHOW:

**The cat**
**Cat box or basket (escape-proof) with newspaper and old blanket in bottom**
**Sanitary tin**
**Litter if needed**
**Clean, warm, plain-white woollen blanket**
**White tape for tally to be worn around cat's neck**
**Non-toxic disinfectant, such as TCP**
**Cotton wool**
**Hot-water bottle (if weather is very cold)**
**Food and water dishes**
**Favourite food**
**Brush and comb**
**Talcum powder in case of accidents (not to be used in hall)**
**Numbered tally**
**Vetting-in and passing-out cards**
**Marked schedule of classes entered.**

For the exhibitor the show day means a very early start. Few shows now allow overnight penning and the vetting-in starts between 7.30 and 8 a.m. on the morning of the show. There is usually a long queue well before this time, awaiting the arrival of the veterinary surgeons who will examine each exhibit individually before they are allowed into the hall. Cats must be taken to the show in an escape-proof container and may not be carried in or led on a harness or lead.

Each vet has a steward who takes the cat out of the basket ready for his examination and takes the vetting-in card to check. As each exhibit is passed, the number is crossed off on the vetting-in board and a small card handed to each owner. This has to be displayed on the pen as proof that the cat has been examined by the vet. Any cat that is considered not fit to be exhibited for some reason or another will not be allowed in. The veterinary surgeon may consider that the kitten is sickening for some infectious disease, is obviously in kitten, is a monorchid or a cryptorchid (not a fully developed adult male), may have sore or inflamed gums, dirty ears, fur full of fleas, or some other condition. If necessary, the temperature is taken. Should the veterinary surgeon consider the cat is not fit to be shown, it is disqualified and must be taken out of the hall and the entry fees forfeited. Shows supply a hospital room where a few pens are put for these cats but as this means they are side by side all day and some may be sickening for some contagious illness, it is far better for the owner to take the cat home. Should the vet consider it necessary, any other exhibits belonging to the same owner may also be banned from the show.

Once through the vetting successfully, the cat must be placed in the pen bearing the same number as the tally around the neck. It is advisable to give the pen a quick wipe over with a little cotton wool dampened with a non-toxic disinfectant or surgical spirit. There will be plain white paper on top of the tabling on which the pen is placed and the warm white blanket you have brought with you should be placed on this. If the weather is very cold, it is permissible to bring a hot-water bottle, provided it is hidden underneath the blanket and cannot be seen. A sanitary tray must also be provided but it should be remembered that a single pen measures $24'' \times 24''$, so it must not be so big that it completely fills the pen, leaving the cat nowhere else to sit. Peat moss is provided by the management for the sanitary trays but many exhibitors prefer to bring a little of the one used by the cat, as peat is inclined to stick to the long fur, spoiling the appearance. Before the cat is put in the pen, a final grooming may be given but powdering is not permitted in the hall and, should the coat be found full of powder, it can mean disqualification. Pens are not decorated in any way, nor hung with curtains as in many shows overseas.

It is better not to feed the cat before the judging. In any case, feeding bowls and any toys must not be put in the pen until after lunch, by which time the open classes will have been judged.

If you are showing two exhibits, care must be taken to ensure that the cat is in the correct pen and has the right tally around the neck. Stewards do check that the numbers are the same, but, once judging has started, it may be difficult to sort things out, to ensure the cats are judged in their right classes. This may lead to disqualification and withholding of the prize money.

Apart from the National Cat Club Show held at the Olympia where the public are admitted all day, the hall will be cleared at about 10 a.m. The public may be allowed to watch from the gallery or from the sides of the hall but this is not always possible.

The judge will go to each pen in turn, accompanied by the steward with table, disinfectant, etc. The steward takes the cat out of the pen and places it on the table for the judging. This goes on all day until all classes are judged. Occasionally a cat will refuse to come out, trying to bite and scratch the steward and the judge may have to pass it by. This does not happen too often but it is not advsiable to bring such a cat to another show.

Soon the results' lists are going up on the award board and by lunch time, when the public are admitted, prize cards begin to appear on the pens. Catalogues are sold, giving the complete names of the exhibits and entries in each class. Check the catalogue as soon as possible to make sure your exhibit is entered in the correct classes and, should there be any queries, see the show manager about these.

The judges will send in their Best in Show, giving the numbers of the cat, kitten and neuter they consider the best. Some shows do not have Best in Show but Best of Breed instead—the best adult and kitten of each variety is chosen, with special rosettes or cards being given to those winners. Should there be Best in Show, these are chosen by selected panels of judges and eventually the best longhaired adult, best longhaired kitten, best shorthaired adult, best shorthaired kitten and the best Siamese cat and kitten, as well as the best neuter from each section, appear in the specially decorated Best in Show pens. The neuters do not compete against the unneutered cats and kittens.

Most of the prize cards are distributed on the day of the show but it may be three to six weeks before the prize money is sent out, as all entries have to be checked by the registrar of the Governing Council of the Cat Fancy to make sure that the details are as stated on the entry forms and reproduced in the catalogue. Disqualification and loss of prize money may follow should errors be discovered.

Most shows close about 6 p.m. The owner may then collect his cat and make his way home, probably feeling quite exhausted but the cat will have to have attention on arrival. It is not advisable to allow any exhibited cat or kitten to run around for the next few days with any others that have been left at home. It may suffer no ill-effects itself but it can still pass on any infection picked up to others. Some fanciers recommend giving a teaspoonful of brandy or whisky in a little milk to the cat and lightly rubbing the fur all over with a piece of cotton wool dampened with a dilution of non-toxic disinfectant, afterwards rubbing dry. The corners of the eyes and inside the ears too may be gently wiped with cotton wool dampened with a little diluted TCP. The cat should then be given a good meal of its favourite food and allowed to settle down for the night but, having been shut up in the pen all day, many chase around quite madly for a while, preferring to play rather than sleep immediately.

## The awards

At British championship shows held under the jurisdiction of the Governing Council of the Cat Fancy, various awards may be given as follows:

The winner of the adult open breed class may be awarded a challenge certificate provided the judge considers the cat to be of high enough standard. The class may be divided into male and female, with both receiving certificates if considered good enough.

Three challenge certificates awarded at three different shows by three separate judges entitle the winner to be known as a champion.

There are also champion of champion classes with the winner of three champion challenge certificates at three shows under three different judges being known as a grand champion. To enter such a class the cat must be a full champion.

A champion cat may be shown in its open breed class and also in the champion of champions class.

There are similar classes for premiers, with the title of grand premier being granted to the winner of the premier of premier certificates at three shows under three separate judges. A premier neuter too may be shown in the open class and also in the premier of premier class but must be a full premier to compete in the latter.

The Governing Council send medals to the new holders of these titles, once proof of winning has been established.

The clubs having Best in Show invariably give splendid rosettes to the winners, while those having Best of Breed instead present bannerettes or rosettes to them as a token of the wins.

The club organizing the show offers very valuable cups, some for members only and some as 'Open Specials'. Certain cups may be won outright eventually, provided certain conditions are complied with—if, for example, a competitor has had five wins with three cats. Others are 'perpetual', which means that the cup or trophy cannot be won outright. However such wins are inscribed on the cup and specials given to commemorate the wins.

The other clubs supporting the show also offer special prizes for their members only; these may take the form of specials commemorating wins on cups, or rosettes.

Cat-food prizes are often offered by the manufacturing firms and small prizes are given for specific wins by private individuals.

After the results have appeared on the award boards, prize cards are eventually put on the winners' pens. A red card signifies a first prize, a blue for second, a yellow for third, green for reserve and white cards for very highly commended, highly commended and commended.

# Chapter seven

# Judging and stewarding

There are those who would like to become judges, those who want only to steward and those who just want to breed and exhibit cats—not to mention those who just like keeping cats, pedigree or not. There is room in the cat world for everyone.

## Appointment of judges

There is no point in aspiring to be a judge unless you are going to enjoy judging and are convinced that you possess that magical quality 'an eye for a cat'. You can only find this out by stewarding for many judges and, by mentally placing the cats before the judge announces her decision, you will be able to tell if your opinion approximates to that of the various judges.

Until now the specialist longhair clubs have appointed the judges for their own breeds. For instance, the Blue Persian Cat Society appointed judges of blue Persians. This meant that the judge so appointed was empowered to judge open classes and award challenge certificates for that particular breed. Judges so appointed had then to be approved by the GCCF. Some clubs stipulated that a judge must serve a probationary period, during which he or she could judge the open kitten classes only, and until this had been done satisfactorily a certain number of times was not allowed to award challenge certificates at championship shows.

Now the Advisory Committee for Longhaired Cats has been formed, composed of representatives from the specialist long-hair clubs. The functions of this committee will include forming a panel of senior longhair judges—three from each of the six founder clubs—and this panel will receive from the specialist clubs the names of proposed new judges and judges seeking promotion from other longhair lists and will now be responsible for appointing these judges.

The six founder clubs are: the Black and White Cat Club, the Blue Persian Cat Society, the Chinchilla, Silver Tabby and Smoke Cat Society, the Colour-point, Rex-Coated, and AOV Club, the Longhair Cream and Blue-Cream Cat Association, the Red, Cream, Tortoiseshell, Tortoiseshell and White, Blue-Cream, and Brown Tabby Society.

To become a judge the candidate must have bred and/or exhibited longhairs for a stipulated period of years and have stewarded a stated number of times, more than half of which must have been with a senior judge of the breed concerned. People who are already judges do not need to qualify in this way but must satisfy the panel that they are competent to judge other varieties.

The intending new judge should apply to the honorary secretary of the Advisory Committee for Longhaired Cats for forms which have to be filled in by the judges for whom the candidate has stewarded. When all conditions have been ful-filled, the candidate applies to the relevant specialist longhair club and at the same time sends a copy of the application together with a fee to the secretary of the Advisory Committee.

## Stewarding

Would-be judges must first serve an apprenticeship as stewards so let us first consider stewarding. The steward is the judge's right-hand man and, before judging even begins, the steward must arrive in good time at the show, find the judge's table, see that the bowl with water and disinfectant and the towel are present, obtain the judges' book from the show manager and check the classes against the schedule, see that the Best in Show slip, lunch tickets etc. are included. The steward must also prepare a card to keep a record of the awards in all the classes (often supplied by the show manager), carry a pencil, pen, and india rubber, find the judge and inform the show manager in case of absence. The steward is also responsible for the judge's table and equipment and carries or pushes it from pen to pen.

Before starting the judge will probably tell the steward how she likes to work. For example, most judges of the open classes like to walk along first looking at each cat in its pen. At this time both judge and steward should mark absentees and it is as well for the steward to check with the show manager that the cats are really absent.

When told to do so the steward takes each cat from its pen, checking that the number on its tally coincides with the pen number. She holds the cat while it is being judged, taking care to present each exhibit in the best possible manner. It is here that the difference between a good and bad steward is most apparent. The design of show pens is by no means perfect and there is considerable art in manoeuvring a large longhair out of a small door so that its temper and coat remain unruffled. A good steward will talk to the cat, handle it gently and soothe it if necessary. It is quite understandable if cats resent strange hands pouncing on them suddenly and dragging them out of their pens, so she should first try to make friends with the cat. At the same time the steward must be prepared for the cat attempting to escape and be ready to tighten her grip. Leave the pen door open while the cat is out being judged, just in case it should panic and have to be returned to the pen very quickly.

When—and not before—the judge indicates that she has finished with the cat put it back in its pen. It is maddening for a judge making notes on a cat to look up and find that the over-eager steward has popped it back.

Some judges explain their reasons for their placings as they go along and others prefer to wait till the end of the class. The good steward speaks when spoken to, at least until she knows the judge well enough to know when it is in order to ask questions.

At the end of the class, the steward marks the placings on her card, checks that the judge has filled in the slips correctly and has signed or initialled all slips. She then takes the two duplicate slips to the table and returns to the judge as quickly as possible, not stopping to chat to friends on the way.

The steward must never attempt to identify the ownership

of cats to the judge and of course she should not steward in any class in which she is exhibiting.

When the judge has finished all her classes, the steward returns the bowl and towel to the show manager and gets the judge's and her own catalogues. There are still the specials to be awarded and this must be done from the catalogue.

The steward's duties are not finished yet. When there is best-in-show judging, all stewards must be available to take the chosen cats up to the table and, when possible, try to contact the owners of the cats and kittens that her judge has nominated for Best in Show so that they can have their baskets ready for the cats to be transported to the platform.

At the best-in-show judging the steward lines up with the other stewards and, when it is her turn, takes the cat out of the basket and hands it to the first judge on the panel. This is the time when cats are most likely to panic, because of the noise and the crowds, so the steward must do all she can to soothe it and give it confidence and be sure it is reasonably calm before passing it to the judge. The steward then takes the basket and goes to the other end of the judges' panel to await the arrival of the cat. Depending on its behaviour, she can then either hold it in her arms until the decision is announced, or if it is worried she can put it back in its basket. Then she either takes it back to its pen, or if it has won Best in Show she puts it in the appropriate pen in front of the platform. Only then is the steward free to attend to her own affairs.

## Judging

Judging cats is not so nearly as easy as one might think from looking at them in the pens. So often a cat looks perfectly lovely sitting on its blanket but if you have it out and examine it thoroughly it can be a totally different story. It may have a kink in its tail, its coat may be very shady or it may have some quite unacceptable fault, such as bars on a chinchilla's legs, or under all the coat it may lack physique. I once had, in an adult male class, an excellent-looking cat viewed from the aisle, only to find he was a monorchid and so had to disqualify him.

The judge must realize that she can only delight one person in each class, although I hasten to add that most exhibitors are good losers. The judge should always be prepared to explain to exhibitors after the judging why she has placed the cats in a particular order.

Every breed has its standard of points and while type is similar in all longhairs, except for Birman and Turkish cats, the number of points allocated to particular characteristics varies for different breeds. In general, when colour or markings are important these rate more highly than the shape of the cat. The GCCF publishes an official booklet called the *Standards of Points* which sets out the standards of all the affiliated specialist clubs. This booklet is a must for all judges, breeders and exhibitors.

The judge must look at each cat in the light of the standard for that particular breed. A few judges award marks for each category (head, coat, etc.) and merely total them up but this does not allow for the overall appearance and balance of the cat's qualities. Most judges prefer to assess the cats mentally, making a note of good and bad points and probably comparing two or three before finally placing them.

The judging book has the left-hand side of every other page divided into three slips by perforations between the first and second and second and third slips. Each slip is divided in two by a line down the centre. On the left-hand side of this line are put the numbers of all the cats in the class with two or three lines between each and the right-hand side is left blank for the judge to write in her placings. On the right-hand page opposite each number the judge writes her comments about each cat.

After the judging, the first two slips are detached from the book and taken by the steward to the show manager's table; one slip is then pinned on the award board. The other is for the show secretary. The third slip remains in the judge's book.

Judges may not exhibit at shows where they are judging and neither may members of their household.

The judge must of course be familiar with the GCCF rules applying to the exhibiting of cats, especially as they apply to her powers. There are various circumstances in which a judge must disqualify a cat—for powder being left in the coat or the coat being trimmed or dyed are examples.

A judge may withhold any prize, including the challenge certificate, if she does not consider the exhibits of sufficient merit to warrant it. If there are less than seven exhibits between the two open breed classes the judge need not award two challenge certificates but may do so if in her opinion the male and female are both worthy of a certificate.

30 **An** outstanding **C**olourpoint champion displaying the many ribbons he has won

31 A proud Chinchilla in Best of Show pen

32 Early morning at the Olympia, the largest cat show in the world

33 A steward holding cat ready for the judge to examine

# Chapter eight

# Cat fancies of the world

---

## North America

The first large cat show was held in Madison Square Gardens in New York, USA, in 1895. Organized by an Englishman, Mr J. Hyde, it followed similar lines to the Crystal Palace shows in Britain and was an immediate success. The Chicago Cat Club was founded in 1899 but was short-lived, being ousted by the Beresford Cat Club founded by Mrs Clinton Locke. It was named after the English breeder, Lady Marcus Beresford, who was interested in so many varieties and frequently exported outstanding cats to the United States.

A year or two later, the American Cat Association came into being as the first registering body, very much in the same manner as did the National Cat Club in Britain. Over the years other associations, clubs and federations have been formed, with a number registering cats and sponsoring shows for their own associated clubs and societies.

These include the Cat Fanciers' Association, founded in 1906. Invariable known as the CFA, it is by far the largest registering body, having more than 400 member clubs and being responsible for more than half the vast number of shows held in America.

The great distances involved in the United States soon made it impracticable to have only one body registering and sponsoring shows and others evolved: 1919 saw the formation of the Cat Fanciers' Federation (CFF); the United Cat Fanciers (UCF) in 1946; the American Cat Fanciers' Association (ACFA) in 1955; the National Cat Fanciers' Association (NCFA) in 1960; the Crown Cat Fanciers' Federation (CCFF) in 1965; and the Independent Cat Federation (ICF) in 1969. The Canadian Cat Association (1961) is exclusively Canadian but several of the other associations hold shows both in the USA and Canada, while the CFA is also associated with certain shows in Japan. There are also a number of clubs not connected with any associations.

Several of the federations have banded together, being collectively known as the International Cat Associations. They accept cats registered with any association at their shows, which helps the exhibitors considerably; otherwise their cats must be registered with each specific organization running the show they wish to enter.

Fortunately the standards accepted are very much the same throughout North America, as is the system of running the shows, which differs considerably from that in Britain.

There are usually four separate shows going on at the same time, with four judges presiding. The judges do not go to the pens but sit at a table in judging rings, with chairs inside for the exhibitors to watch the judging.

The cats are vetted-in and taken to the cages by the owners, who bring curtains to hang inside in colours complimentary to the cats and put a thick coloured blanket or cushion in the bottom for the cat to sit on. Litter trays, food and water are usually provided by the management.

The classes that can be entered are few. The important ones are: the novice class for cats who have never won as an adult; the open class for those who already have a recorded win; the champion for cats that hold four winners' ribbons; and grand champions—the winner of the latter class is decided on a points' basis and on the number of other champions beaten. The classes are divided into 'colour' or variety classes and into male and female. Some associations have awards for the best cat in show, second best cat, best opposite-sex cat, best or opposite-sex champion and grand champion. The CFA has a more simple arrangement now and chooses the five best cats.

When judging starts, the owner is called and takes the cat to the judge's table. The judge examines the cat thoroughly and the cat is then put in one of the ten empty pens behind her, while she marks up her judging sheet. She puts ribbons on the cages of the winners, blue, unlike in Britain, being the first-prize colour, with red for second.

Once a cat has been beaten it is returned to its own cage but the winners are judged against each other until eventually the best cat is found. As in all probability four shows are going on at the same time in different rings, a cat may have been entered in the others and will be judged by a different judge, the system being exactly the same. It is therefore possible eventually for the same cat to be best in all the rings; on the other hand there may be four best cats chosen.

A kitten must be four months old to be shown in a kitten class and at eight months is considered to be old enough to enter the adult class.

The judges are paid according to the number of exhibits judged and receive travelling and hotel expenses. In Britain the judges give their services free, receiving only travelling expenses and hotel expenses for one night should this be required.

Would-be judges have to undergo an intensive training programme before being considered as a possible judge. This varies slightly from one organization to another but is always broadly similar. Any applicants must have been associated with the association for a set number of years and must have bred at least one cat which has come best, or near best, in a show. They must have had experience of clerking at shows, attend courses and give practical demonstrations in the handling and judging of cats, under the guidance of accepted judges. They start as trainees, then become apprentices, then approval-pending judges and, depending on the ratings received, their answers in written examinations and approval being given by the board of the association, may become specialty judges. By further work and study they may eventually become all-breed judges.

In Canada the first recorded show was held in Toronto in 1906, sponsored by the Royal Canadian Cat Club but it was not until 1961 that the Canadian Cat Association started registering cats for the first time in Canada.

There had been a great deal of interest in cats before this date and many cat clubs were already in existence but the cats were registered with one of the American organizations. The 1939–45 war saw, as in Britain, almost the complete cessation of pedigree cat breeding and cat shows but things started up again shortly after the war ended, with a number of breeders soon producing excellent kittens once again. Shows were held once more, with the Royal National Cat Club sponsoring the important shows held at the Canadian National Exhibition, an annual exhibition including shows for all kinds of animals. In 1968 the Canadian National Cat Club was disbanded and the Royal Canadian Cat Club took over the responsibility for the cat show at the Exhibition.

Shows in Canada are run on similar lines to those in the United States and both countries participate freely in each other's cat activities. Cats from Canada may be shown in the United States, and *vice versa*, judges from both countries often officiating at the same show.

Interest in pedigree cats increases each year in Canada, with more and more clubs coming into being and more shows being held.

Generally the shows in the United States and Canada are not as large as those held in the British Isles but the distances to be travelled are very great and many exhibitors go by plane for quickness, although others travel many hundred of miles by car. The shows are usually two-day affairs.

For exhibitors showing cats both in Canada and the USA, there is the added excitement of winning one of the much-coveted awards, that of International Champion and International Grand Champion. A cat must be a champion or a grand champion in each country to achieve this feat.

## Europe

It was in the 1890s in Paris that the first cat shows were held in France. These early shows attracted much attention and many people became interested in breeding pedigree cats but the numbers have never reached British levels, for example. The longhairs and, more recently, the Siamese have been the most popular, although all varieties are now seen at the shows, some being imported from Britain and America.

The Netherlands is probably the most cat-minded with Belgium and France following closely behind. Germany's first cat show was held in 1924 and there are now regular shows, while Switzerland had its first show in Geneva in 1933 and now has several each year. Although there are Italian judges who officiate all over Europe, very few shows are held in that country. More recently Czechoslovakia has shown interest in cats and there is now a club affiliated to FIFE.

FIFE (the *Fédération Internationale Féline de Europe*) is the largest governing body in Europe, having a number of clubs and associations affiliated to it. More than 12 countries can participate in their shows, including the Scandinavian countries and most mainland European ones.

There are also the independent associations, which register cats. These are the *Union des Associations Félines de France* presided over by Madame M. Lochet; and the *Cercle Féline de Paris* whose president is the Baronne de Saint-Palais. The clubs attached to these organizations run shows in Paris and other parts of France, with entries coming from all over Europe.

The Netherlands showed interest early on in the century with a number of people owning pedigree cats but there were no shows as such. In the 1920s, Dutch fanciers took their cats to the show in Antwerp, Belgian, to the show organized by *Les Amis du Chat*, the first cat club in Europe, founded as long ago as 1917.

An exhibition was held in Rotterdam in 1928 but the first cat club, *Felicat*, was not found until 1934, with their first show being held in the same year in Haarlem.

At first the majority of cats seen at the shows were all long-haired and it was not until the late 1950s that the shorthairs began to come into their own.

After the 1939–45 war it took many years for the Dutch Cat Fancy to recover but there are now several independent clubs as well as those affiliated to FIFE, all of which hold annual shows. The Dutch are very keen on new varieties and imports from all parts of the world appear on the show benches there.

Belgium too has several cat clubs and also holds a number of shows each year. The Antwerp Cat Club, the oldest in Europe, holds an annual show under the able management of Madame L. Dekesel. Shows are also held in Brussels.

In Scandinavia there are a number of cat clubs with shows being held annually. It is difficult for some fanciers to keep many cats as, owing to the severe winters, particularly in Norway and Sweden, they cannot be allowed outside. Cat shows were held early in the 1920s but it was not until 1931 that the first cat club was founded, the Danish *Race Katte Klubb* and there are now several others affiliated to FIFE. The founding of a club in Norway, the *Kattevennes Klubb*, came in 1934 and was quickly followed by others. There are also independent clubs there.

Sweden's first club was started in 1946 and is affiliated to FIFE and there are also several independent clubs, such as the *Sveriges Nye Raskattklubb* and *Gastriklands nya Rastkattklubb*.

In the 1960s the *Sunomen Rotukissayhoistys r.y. (Surok)*—Finland's first cat club—came into being and shows are now held there regularly too.

It is possible for all the European countries to have international shows and subsequently international champions, as, unlike in Britain, quarantine regulations are not involved, although should there be an outbreak of some infectious disease, such as rabies, restrictions may be enforced, with vaccinations and injections being compulsory before a cat may attend a show in another country.

The shows in Europe are usually held for two days, with the cats being taken to hotels overnight. All exhibitors must be members of the club organizing the show. Pens may be hung with curtains and decorated with the ribbons and rosettes won at previous shows, while the cats often sit on satin and velvet cushions and may have vases of flowers beside them. The colours are chosen to show the cats off to their best. The cats are not penned in varieties, as in Britain, but in 'families'—the cats belonging to the same exhibitor may be penned together in the same cage or next to one another. The numbers do not run in rotation but the stewards study the hall penning plan before going to find a particular cat.

The method of judging is very much the same as that in America. The stewards take the cats to the judge who sits at a table in a side room ready to examine them. There will be a row of pens behind her, should she wish to compare certain cats, but she does not give ribbons, as in America, nor does the cat remain until beaten. The classes are few in number and there are now clubs' classes as in Britain. One show in Paris, however, does prefer to use the same judging methods as the British, with the judges going to the pens.

The spectators and exhibitors stay in the hall all day, many sitting beside their pens. Judging is usually completed on the first day, with the best exhibits being chosen on the second. There is no prize money but each winner is presented with a banner or a prize in kind, with the Best-in-Show winners getting most splendid rosettes. Each entry receives a card, which is hung on the pen, that indicates the qualification given: excellent, very good, or good, and that a prize was won or not. The card is signed by the judge concerned.

The following are the awards to be won: CAC, the *Certificat d'Aptitude de Championnat*, which is equivalent to a challenge certificate and CACIB, the *Certificat d'Aptitude de Championnat International de Beauté*. This requires three CACs to be awarded in three different countries before a cat may become an international champion.

Many British judges officiate at European shows and are usually most impressed with the high quality of some of the exhibits. There are a number of European judges, some of whom are also on British lists and may officiate at shows in Britain. To become a judge in Europe one must steward for a number of times and be a pupil judge at least six times, eventually taking an oral and written examination conducted by two fully qualified judges.

Many international friendships have originated through meetings at cat shows throughout the world and now a number of cat clubs organize charter flights for their members to visit the most important cat shows in various countries.

## Australia and New Zealand

It is more than 70 years since the first pedigree longhaired cats arrived in Australia from Britain to form the foundations of the Cat Fancy there. From a slow start the interest in cat breeding has increased so much over the years that now every state has a Cat Fancy, loosely connected with one another but in most cases working quite independently.

The very size of the country makes it necessary for each state to have its own governing body—in some cases more than one. In some states the Cat Fancies are governed by the Royal Agricultural Societies and Feline Control Councils of the area. There are seven areas in all, each having a separate register for the cats. New South Wales, the first to have a Cat Fancy, is unique in that it registers cats from other states as well as its own.

The registrations, show organization and judging methods are very much the same throughout the country, having been based on those instituted by the Governing Council in Britain in the first place.

There are many clubs, each affiliated to or controlled by their state's governing body. Shows are held all the year round, some clubs running more then one. The average entry is from 200 to 300 cats and kittens, with one large show in New South Wales attracting over 1,000.

The show procedure is as for Britain, with vetting-in before entry into the hall and the judges going to the cages with their stewards to take out and examine the cats.

Australian judges have a very thorough training, attending courses and taking examinations before being permitted to judge. Judges may officiate at shows in states other than their own and, as in North America, many travel enormous distances to judge at specific shows. Many exhibitors travel with their cats to the shows by air.

The longhaired varieties are as recognized in Britain, with the addition of the shaded silvers and some are outstanding in type with good coats. The cameos too are making good progress. There is still a regular importation of outstanding stock from Britain of most varieties; the blues, creams and whites are particularly favoured.

New Zealand has a very active Cat Fancy with both islands being controlled by the Governing Council of the Cat Fancy of New Zealand. There are a number of shows each year, with the largest having an entry of 600 cats, being sponsored by one of the pet-food organizations and run by a different club at a different venue each year.

The rules and regulations regarding registrations, shows and judges are much the same as in Britain.

Generally the standard of the longhairs is becoming increasingly high and some magnificent specimens may be seen at the shows.

There are no quarantine restrictions between Australia and New Zealand and there are frequent importations of cats between the two countries.

## South Africa

South Africa started later than most countries in the development of a Cat Fancy but one is now in full swing. There are five clubs, which together formed the Governing Council of the Associated Cat Clubs of South Africa in 1970. All registrations and transfers are dealt with by the South African Cat Register.

As in Australia, the judges attend courses and take written examinations, eventually becoming all-round judges.

Shows are held frequently and are run on similar lines to those of the British. Most clubs own their own pens and set up the shows, doing all the work themselves. Again, because of the size of the country, both judges and exhibitors travel frequently by air to the shows.

## Britain

### THE GOVERNING COUNCIL

The Governing Council of the Cat Fancy (GCCF) is composed of delegates elected annually by members of the individual affiliated cat clubs and societies.

Of the many affiliated clubs and societies throughout the British Isles some are specialist clubs dealing with all matters relating to specific varieties, such as the Blue Persian Cat Society or the Black and White Cat Club, whilst others are known as all-breed clubs, being interested in all varieties. All are represented on the Council.

The Council approves registration of cats, cat pedigrees and transfers from one owner to another. It discusses and advises on various matters regarding cat welfare, approves and classifies cat breeds and grants prefixes. It also deals with matters regarding cat shows, approving the dates of the championship, sanction and exemption shows held annually under its auspices and run according to its regulations and rules. Challenge and premier certificates are given by the Council at the championship shows if the judges decide the cats there are up to the desired standard.

Its various publications include a stud book published every year or so, an annual stud list, lists of cat shows, cat clubs, approved standard of points and a judges' list.

The whole Council meet an average of four times a year but there are various sub-committees, each with specific duties, such as the executive, which meets nearly every month, finance, disciplinary, constitution and the cat-care committees.

It is not always realized that after each approved cat show, the show manager has to submit marked catalogues to the secretary. These are checked by the registrars to make sure there are no errors in the entries before the prize money is paid out.

The delegates give their services voluntarily, the Council having only a small paid staff, consisting of the secretary and several registrars. The Council elects its own president, chairman, assistant chairman and treasurer and also those who serve on the various sub-committees.

The GCCF could not exist at all were it not for the cat clubs; the cat clubs could not exist without members and it is these members with common interests, such as the breeding and showing of cats and looking after their well-being that make up the ever-increasing, world-wide Cat Fancy.

The secretary of the GCCF lives at Dovefields, Petworth Road, Witley, Surrey. Any correspondence requiring a reply should be accompanied by a stamped addressed envelope.

CLUBS AND SOCIETIES

There are more than 50 cat clubs and societies in Britain, the majority being all-breed clubs, which are for cat fanciers interested in any or all varieties. Some are known as specialist clubs being solely for those interested in specific varieties. The clubs mainly of interest to admirers of longhaired cats are as follows:

Birman Cat Club
Black and White Cat Club
Blue Persian Cat Society
Capital Longhair Cat Association
Chinchilla Silver and Smoke Society
Colour-point Rex-Coated and AOV Club
Colour-point Society of Great Britain
Longhaired Cat Club
Longhair Cream and Blue-Cream Association
North of Britain Longhair Cat Club
Red-Cream, Tortoiseshell, Tortoiseshell and White, Blue-Cream and Brown Tabby Society.
Tabby Cat Club
White Persian Cat Club

As secretaries and their addresses may change frequently, it is not sensible to give addresses but for a full list of clubs with their names and addresses, application should be made to the secretary of the Governing Council of the Cat Fancy, Dovefields, Petworth Road, Witley, Surrey, enclosing a stamped addressed envelope and 10p.

WELFARE SOCIETIES

There are a number of British animal welfare societies concerned with the well-being of animals, including cats. There is only one that deals exclusively with cats, and this is the Cats' Protection League, whose head office is at 29, Church Street, Slough, Bucks, England. There are also various branches throughout the country.

The CPL, as it is known, will arrange for the spaying and neutering of cats and kittens not required for breeding. The owners pay as much as they can afford for this service which is performed by qualified veterinary surgeons, with the League paying the balance. They are also always trying to find good homes for unwanted cats and kittens.

The Blue Cross Society, whose Head Office is at 1, Hugh Street, Victoria, London, England, runs a number of clinics and hospitals throughout Britain, where treatment may be given free to sick cats whose owners are unable to pay the fees. They also try to find good homes for stray and unwanted cats and kittens.

The People's Dispensary for Sick Animals (PDSA) has a number of permanent and mobile dispensaries throughout the country. The head office is at South Street, Dorking, Surrey, England. The PDSA will give treatment to sick animals whose owners cannot afford private veterinary fees.

The Royal Society for the Prevention of Cruelty to Sick Animals (RSPCSA) has clinics in most towns in England and Wales. Their inspectors deal with complaints of cruelty to animals including cats; the addresses may be found in the local telephone directory. The clinics give free veterinary treatment and advice on cats to owners that cannot afford to pay fees. The RSPCA also has boarding kennels.

Most of these organizations issue pamphlets on the care of cats, which they will send out on receipt of a stamped addressed envelope. There may also be a small charge involved. They are all voluntary bodies dependent on donations, as are a number of other organizations throughout the country, mostly local, which will arrange for the spaying of cats and also give treatment and advice in times of sickness. It is impossible to give the names and addresses of them all.

CATS AND BRITISH LAW

From time to time it has been suggested that cats should be licensed in the same way as dogs but, although much thought has been given to it, so far it has been thought to be impracticable as it is felt that the wandering nature of the cat would make it very difficult to enforce the measure and would be responsible probably for an even greater increase in the number of strays about.

Licences are not required to keep a cat or a cattery but are required for boarding catteries, which have first to be inspected by the local authorities.

Cats are not protected by law as adequately as one would like but are covered by a number of animal acts which provide that:

1. Anyone ill-treating a cat in any way may be prosecuted, as may anyone knowingly poisoning or administering poisonous drugs to a cat.

2. A cat may not be shot for trespass alone, as the owner is not liable if a cat, following its natural instincts, trespasses, kills fowls and so on, or digs up plants.

3. A general anaesthetic must be administered when neutering a cat over six months and for any severe operation.

4. Anyone knowingly injuring a cat in an accident must do something to relieve its suffering.

5. All animals which have value and are the property of any person are protected against theft.

6. Licensing and inspection of all pet shops is required and there are conditions governing the accommodation and care of the animals offered for sale. No child under 12 may purchase a pet.

7. Anyone abandoning an animal in circumstances liable to cause suffering may be prosecuted under the Abandonment of Animals Act.

Chapter nine

# Cat health

## Nursing

When a cat is seriously ill, sympathetic nursing is quite as important as medical treatment. Although the cat does not like to be bothered and fussed over, often the right kind of care makes all the difference to the outcome of the illness. Sometimes, when the cat is feeling so ill that it doesn't care whether it gets better or not the owner, by establishing an emotional bond, can boost the cat's morale and give it the will to live. I have seen cats (and other animals) lie down and die from some comparatively minor illness simply because they lacked the incentive to get better and the owner was unable to provide it. In fact, in the case of a Pekingese who had to have a necessary but straight-forward operation the owner was so convinced beforehand that the bitch would die as a result of it, that die she did some days later, for no apparent physical reason.

Whether the cat is to be nursed in a cattery or indoors it should have a comfortable bed—a cardboard box with a soft blanket in it will do very well—and a warm atmosphere with adequate ventilation ensuring a supply of fresh air without draughts. The bed should be shaded from full daylight or artificial light, otherwise the cat may creep out to find a dark spot. The sanitary tray should be within easy reach of the bed. If the cat is not accustomed to using a tray, it will have to be carried out to the garden to its favourite spot and taken indoors again as soon as it has finished. This is better than allowing the animal to become constipated or having too full a bladder. You will have to be careful that it does not escape and is not allowed out without supervision until convalescent. A very sick cat may feel the urge to crawl under a bush to die and you might be unable to find it in time because it certainly won't come when called.

Follow your veterinary surgeon's instructions regarding medicines and feeding; there is usually a reason for any specific do's and dont's. You will know best what titbits are likely to tempt your cat to eat but in some cases certain foods may be contra-indicated. For instance a cat suffering from jaundice should not have fat in any form, so it is of no use thinking that a little cream is just the thing to give pussy. It will do more harm than good.

Unless medicines have to be given at certain hours, there is no need to disturb a sleeping animal to give it a pill or change a dressing. Much better for it to sleep as much as possible.

When a cat has been ill and off its food you may find difficulty in coaxing it to start eating again, even when convalescent. Try offering it strongly flavoured morsels such as liver sausage or sardines, or something which it does not normally eat like cake or bread and butter. Cats seem to fancy something different, so try little titbits of whatever you are eating yourself. I once had a queen who had not eaten for a week and turned up her nose at everything she was offered. I handed her a piece of Yorkshire pudding which to my surprise was rapidly eaten and more demanded—as if I should have known that was the one thing she had been waiting for.

It is also worth-while leaving a little food near the patient all night; some cats will eat after dark and when no one is about. Another tip is to let the cat smell the food cooking, to stimulate the salivary glands. Contrary as they are, cats may not eat if they think you are over-anxious about it, so do not be constantly offering food—leave a decent interval between attempts.

Longhair coats naturally get in a mess when the cat is ill, not only with spilt medicine and food but also because the coat quickly loses condition and the cat is unfit to cope with it. The amount of grooming you can do depends on how ill the cat is and whether it feels able to bear with it. At least keep its mouth and chest clean by wiping with damp cotton wool and drying with a piece of soft towelling. If the cat has diarrhoea it may be necessary to clip the hair round the anus and down the hind legs. Also wash any soiled fur gently with warm water, dry and apply talcum powder to the fur and a little vaseline to the anus.

Some cats like to have a well-wrapped-up, hot-water bottle to lie on or beside, others do not. An infra-red heater suspended over the bed is also appreciated. If gastritis or enteritis is a part of the illness you may find that the cat will seek out a cold surface to lie on. This should be prevented by confining the cat in a travelling basket. In this case do not make it uncomfortable by putting it on a warm blanket or under a source of heat. Use newspaper for bedding and just make sure that the room temperature is high enough so that the cat doesn't get chilled.

As soon as the patient is well enough, and provided your veterinary surgeon agrees, let the cat be outdoors for some time each day, but not of course in damp weather. A walk in the garden cheers up a cat by stimulating its interest in life. It may have become very bored sitting in its sickroom all day.

INFECTIOUS ILLNESS

If the illness is infectious or contagious the patient must be isolated from all other susceptible animals and humans. It is easiest if one person can attend the sick animal and another the healthy ones and of course the nurse must keep right away from all uninfected cats. Keep an overall and headscarf at the entrance to the sick room to put on as you go in and also an old pair of shoes. Put a shallow tray of water and disinfectant at the door and stand in it before taking off the shoes. Use plenty of disinfectant to wash your hands frequently; if allergic to it wear rubber or plastic gloves. Make your arrangements in the room as complete as possible and include washing facilities, so that you do not carry germs out of it. Anything taken out of the infected area must be destroyed or disinfected immediately and it is a good idea to keep a supply of polythene bags handy, then anything so removed can be popped into one and there is thus no chance of infected material contaminating the 'clean' area.

DISEASES COMMON TO CATS AND HUMANS

A few diseases are communicable from cat to man and obviously the converse is also true. So it is always advisable to wash your hands after grooming even the apparently healthy cat and more so after handling a sick animal.

The diseases which are common to cat and human are:

*Salmonellosis*—a gastro-enteric infection with symptoms of vomiting, diarrhoea and dysentery. Can be serious so take extra precautions when the cat has diarrhoea.

*Tuberculosis*—rare nowadays.

*Toxoplasmosis*—thought to be transmissible and, according to one researcher, may cause pregnant women to abort.

*Rabies*—thanks to our quarantine regulations this is not a risk in this country but, in countries where rabies is prevalent, the bite of a rabid cat will transmit the disease which is always fatal to man unless a series of injections are given in time.

*Mange*—the mite of cat mange seldom affects the human and is not very troublesome when it does.

*Ringworm*—highly contagious. Wear gloves when handling an affected animal.

*Fleas*—cat fleas may bite some people but soon leave the human for a more acceptable host.

*Lice*—I can find no evidence of cat lice being found on people.

*Cheyletiella parasitivorax*—a rabbit mite sometimes found on the cat, it causes an itchy rash on some humans.

ADMINISTERING MEDICINE

Where the cat is concerned this is more easily said than done. If it means a prolonged struggle every time with frayed tempers on both sides this does a very sick cat no good at all. Quite often it will be possible for your veterinary surgeon to give a drug by injection instead and this would be preferable, even if it means the extra expense of daily visits.

Before attempting to give any medicine, it is essential for the cat to be immobilized. Not only does this save you from scratches but, more important perhaps, it prevents the cat from exhausting itself by struggling. If the cat is fairly docile it will probably be enough for an assistant to sit the cat on a table, stand behind it, hold its body between her forearms and grasp one front leg in each hand, high up the leg so that the cat cannot use either shoulder or elbow joint. She must keep a firm grip because if the animal feels itself controlled it is less likely to attempt to struggle. This method is satisfactory for dosing

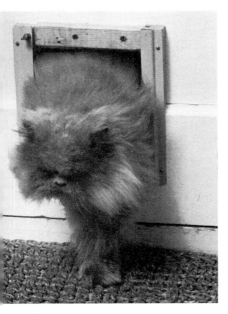

34 Cat showing how to use door flap

35 A Chinchilla enjoying her daily grooming

36 A Blue having her eye cleaned gently with dampened cotton wool

37 The ear of a Blue being cleaned with cotton wool swab

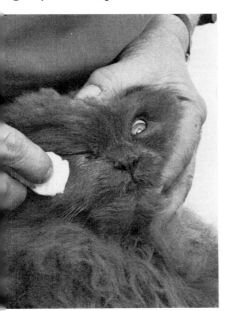

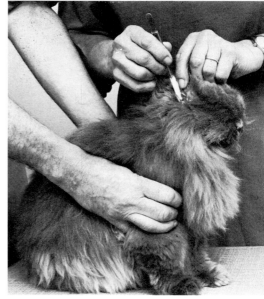

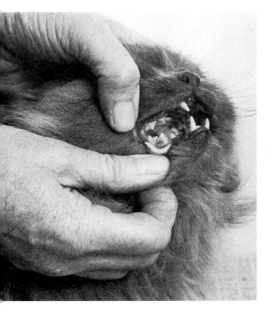

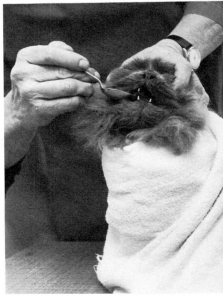

38 Examining the teeth for presence of tartar

39 Cat wrapped correctly in towel ready for administration of medicine

40 Cat's nails being clipped. This is best attended to by a veterinary surgeon

41 Taking the temperature, which should be done with great care, preferably only by a veterinary surgeon

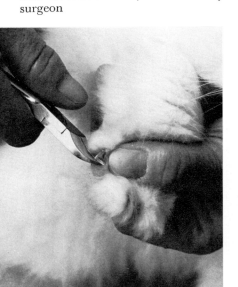

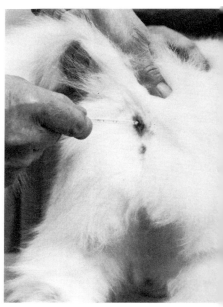

with tablets or capsules but when liquids have to be given then the next method is better as it saves the cat's fur from becoming soiled and greasy. Lay a thickish towel or blanket flat on the table, sit the cat on it, bring one long side of the towel up under the cat's chin and wrap first one end and then the other tightly over its back. Tuck any loose ends under the cat. The assistant then holds the bundled-up cat between her forearms as before, keeping the towel fixed round the cat's neck so that it cannot wriggle its forelegs free. A handy method is to make a bag out of an old blanket, putting a drawstring round the mouth of the bag. Put the cat in tail first leaving its head out and tighten the drawstring round the neck, of course being careful not to strangle it.

LIQUID MEDICINE

Unless palatable, it is impossible to administer a liquid to most cats. Although you may manage to get it into the cat's mouth, instead of swallowing the cat will produce copious amounts of froth and sit there with strings of saliva and medicine pouring from its mouth. If any is swallowed it is liable to be vomited. You will probably have to give nourishment, rather than medicine, in liquid form and this is more likely to be acceptable to the patient.

Having got the cat firmly wrapped up or in the bag as already explained, grasp the head in your left hand with the thumb and first finger under the cheek bones, then tilt the head backwards, at the same time stretching the neck a little. In this manner you will find the cat is less able to clench its teeth. The liquid can be in a dropper or a pointed teaspoon. Pour a little in the side of the mouth through the teeth and allow the cat to swallow. At any sign of choking release the head instantly. I prefer to use a teaspoon because I can depress the lower jaw slightly with the point, thus allowing the liquid to run in more freely.

SOLID MEDICINE

This is usually in tablet form. Powders are not usually acceptable to cats, causing them to salivate profusely and if they have to be given are better put into a gelatin capsule. Empty

L

capsules can be obtained from a chemist. If tasteless, powders or crushed-up tablets can be mixed in a favourite food.

Hold the cat's head in your left hand, in the same manner as when giving liquids; hold the tablet or capsule between your right forefinger and thumb; with your middle finger open the cat's mouth by pressing on the lower jaw between the fangs; pop the tablet as far down the throat as you can; hold the mouth shut, keeping the head slightly raised until the cat swallows. Remember the quickness of the hand deceives the cat, so be as expeditious as you can and never put your fingers between the upper and lower fangs or you are liable to get a painful bite. If the cat does not swallow and spits the pill out, repeat the process. The secret is to get the pill as far to the back of the tongue as you can—push it with the handle of a teaspoon or the blunt end of a pencil if necessary. Should the cat get the taste of the pill, especially a bitter taste, it will produce strings of saliva and champ its jaws as if it were having a fit. Do not be alarmed; this will gradually pass off. The trouble is that after this has happened the very sight of a pill or medicine bottle is liable to start the cat salivating and it is then very difficult to administer any medicine. In any case, cats very quickly spot what you are doing, so hide the medicine until the last moment and never let cats see you putting medicine in their food—they very soon realize what is happening.

TAKING THE TEMPERATURE

The average body temperature of the cat is 100.4°–101°F (38°C), while for kittens it is usually slightly higher. Placing the thermometer in the groin or armpit is too hit or miss a method and in any case only records the temperature on the surface of the body. The deep body temperature is the significant one. For this a stub-ended thermometer is inserted in the rectum. Either wrap the cat up tightly or get a helper to hold it; lubricate the bulb of the thermometer with soap or oil; hold the base of the tail with the left hand and, gently pressing on the anus, gradually insert the thermometer for at least half an inch into the rectum. Hold in place for one minute.

It should not too often be necessary for the owner to take the cat's temperature. A rise of temperature is not necessarily significant unless correlated with other symptoms. If an ailing cat fights against the temperature-taking and struggles violently it only exhausts itself. So in this case leave the job to your veterinary surgeon to do if he thinks it necessary.

## First aid

### ROAD ACCIDENTS

Here you are dealing with an animal which is in a state of shock to a greater or lesser degree and probably with some injury. The essential requirements are warmth and immobilization and self-discipline on the part of the owner. Hysterics will not help the cat, however shattered you may feel. Approach the cat with caution—the most sweet-tempered animal is liable to lash out at anyone who comes near when it is in pain. Cover it in a thick blanket, roll it up gently and put it in a travelling basket if you have one handy. For those who keep cats it is a good plan always to have a basket available for use in an emergency. Telephone your veterinary surgeon and arrange either to take the cat to him or for him to call. Do not take the cat to a surgery unless you are sure there is someone in attendance. You may waste a lot of time driving round all the vets in the district trying to find one available, so telephone first.

Do not attempt to do anything yourself except to keep the cat warm and still unless there is haemorrhage, in which case, try to arrest it. If the blood is just oozing this does not matter too much unless excessive. But if the blood is bright red and spurting out this is an arterial haemorrhage and must be stopped. Apply pressure to the bleeding site either by a wad of cotton wool bandaged tightly on or, if this is impossible, by digital pressure. Unless massive, haemorrhage is not usually a serious problem in cat accidents and is probably not as bad as you think. Remember a little blood goes a long way and that a haemorrhage tends to stop.

### POISONING

If you actually see the cat eat a poison, as may happen with slug-bait and some rat or mouse poisons which are palatable, give it an emetic at once. Either push down a small knob of washing soda or administer salt and water. After the cat has been sick take it for veterinary treatment. Do not give an emetic if the poison is an irritant or has burned the mouth. Milk or beaten white of egg may be given. More commonly cats inadvertently lick poisons such as weedkillers off their coats and feet while grooming themselves and you will not realize what has happened until symptoms appear.

Amongst the symptoms of poisoning are: vomiting, muscular twitching, panting, staggering, fits and abdominal pain.

Get veterinary treatment as quickly as you can and if possible take with you the container of the suspected poison. The label may tell you the antidote but nowadays many weedkillers and rat poisons do not have a specific antidote and it is just a case of treating the symptoms.

One type of poisoning which you can guard against is Warfarin poison. If you know that it has been used in your neighbourhood give your cats a Vitamin K tablet daily until all danger is past. It is not necessary for the cat to have had access to the Warfarin—it can be affected by eating a poisoned rat or mouse.

### BITES AND FIGHTS

Most cats will at some time in their lives be involved in a fight with another cat, or even just a minor disagreement with their normal companions. The injury inflicted is usually a punctured wound which frequently develops into an abscess. (This is discussed in more detail later.) This wound is inflicted by either the claw or the fang of the opponent and may be quite deep, because of the length and sharpness of the weapon. In the longhair cat such wounds are very difficult to find but a tuft of damp hair (caused by slight bleeding or a serous exudate) may give a clue to the location. So if you see or hear a cat quarrel (and they are seldom silent), examine the cat or cats immediately, before grooming can remove the evidence. Having found a puncture, clip the hair around the area, bathe with warm water and mild disinfectant and apply antibiotic ointment to and into the wound. Repeat two or three times daily until healed.

## BURNS

Because cats like to be around when cooking is taking place, either because of the good smells or the warmth from the stove, it is not uncommon for them to be scalded by hot liquids. Having caught and restrained the cat, pour cold water on the burn immediately—but not in sufficient quantity to souse the cat. Clip the hair from around the burn, apply a cold compress if you can, wrap the cat up warmly because it will be shocked and get veterinary treatment as soon as possible. Do not put oily or greasy dressings on the burn.

Sometimes a cat will jump on the stove and burn the pads of its foot. In this case plunge the leg in a jug of cold water and keep it there for a few minutes, then proceed as above.

## BONE IN THE THROAT

When feeding your cat cooked fish, rabbit, hare or chicken, try to remove all the bones, particularly the small ones, because it is these which are liable to get stuck in the cat's mouth or throat. Larger bones are seldom troublesome.

If the bone is stuck in the mouth, say between the teeth or jammed across the hard palate, the cat will claw frantically at its mouth and probably salivate. Get someone to hold the cat wrapped tightly in a blanket with just its head protruding. Hold the head in your left hand as for administering a pill, tilt the head back and with a pair of tweezers grasp the bone firmly and work it loose.

If the bone is stuck in the throat the cat will refuse all food, sit huddled in a corner and probably have strings of saliva hanging from its mouth. It may also try to vomit. This is a job for the veterinary surgeon. Do not attempt to remove the bone yourself—you may only make matters worse by pushing the bone further down the oesophagus or causing the cat to choke.

## CUTS

A small cut will heal quite satisfactorily, provided the cat does not lick it excessively. Some cats simply cannot leave a wound alone, and although it is generally better for wounds to be exposed to the air, if the cat is making the cut raw and weepy by licking or scratching constantly you will have to take action to prevent it. You can either bandage the part or, if this is not possible, then as a last resort an Elizabethan collar can be used. This is fairly uncomfortable to wear and many cats will not tolerate it, nearly going mad in their efforts to remove it. To make one, take a piece of fairly pliable cardboard and cut out in the shape of a collar. Lace up the holes with string in the manner of a shoe lace. Do not forget to remove the collar to allow the cat to eat and drink.

A cut more than about half an inch in length will probably need to be sutured.

### PETROL, PARAFFIN, PAINT AND TAR

Petrol and paraffin oil, especially the latter, are quite often trodden in accidentally by cats and quick action is required to remove it before the cat can lick its paws and by so doing burn its mouth with the contaminant. However quick you are, there is still likely to be some swelling and inflammation of the pads, because the cat's skin is exceptionally sensitive to these oils.

Wash the feet with a bland soap and warm water, rinse well and repeat the process several times until all smell has gone. Finally, dry the feet and apply either talcum powder or a soothing lotion. If the pads are reddened and swollen or the mouth is burnt, get veterinary treatment.

Wet paint is a hazard for longhaired cats—they can so easily brush against it unintentionally—so when you are doing any decorating around the house, remember to exclude the cat. The only satisfactory way to remove paint from a cat's coat is to cut the hair. On no account use turpentine as cats are just as sensitive to it as to paraffin oil. It may be possible to remove some paint while it is still wet with crumpled kitchen paper.

On hot days tar macadam on roads melts and a cat may tread in it. To remove, work some lard well into the tar until it is all blended then wash off with soap and water. You may have to do this several times until all the tar is removed. This is a very messy business, so put on an overall and sit the patient on newspaper.

Ailments: common symptoms and some possible causes

Longhaired cats are quite as healthy bodily as any other variety, including non-pedigree cats. Keeping their long coats in good order is really the only difference between them and any other cat and so ailments, diseases and treatments are basically the same for all.

In the following list of symptoms and their likely causes, it is not suggested that the owner should diagnose the trouble except in the case of something simple. For instance, scratching caused by external parasites.

APPETITE, LOSS OF (*anorexia*)
Occurs in almost every disease and is usually the first indication that the cat is unwell

CATARRH
Viral respiratory diseases (in the chronic stage)
Sinusitis
Foreign body in nostril

CONSTIPATION
Dietetic errors
Foreign body in intestine
Intussusception (telescoping of the bowel)
Sometimes seen in feline infectious enteritis
Old age, owing to slowing down of bowel movements

COUGHING
Viral respiratory diseases
Bronchitis
Pulmonary emphysema
Roundworms
Furball
Laryngitis
Pneumonia

DIARRHOEA
Dietetic—frequently caused by cow's milk
Feline infectious enteritis
Coccidiosis in kittens
Enteric bacteria
Poisoning
Worms

**EYES, THIRD LID SHOWING**
One eye affected—foreign body in eye; tumour of the haw
Both eyes affected—tapeworm infestation; general debility

**EYES, WEEPY**
Viral respiratory diseases
Overtype—if constant and cat is not unwell
Entropion (turned-in eyelids)
Irritant substance such as powder

**HEAD, HELD ON ONE SIDE**
Ear mites
Haematoma
Middle-ear disease
Stroke

**HEAD, SHAKING OF**
Ear mites
Foreign body in ear

**LAMENESS**
Abscess
Strain
Ingrowing nail
Fracture
Dislocation

**SCRATCHING**
Matted or dead hair
Fleas, lice, ticks, harvest mites
Ringworm
Mange
Allergy
Eczema

**SNEEZING**
Viral respiratory diseases
Allergy
Foreign body such as a grass awn in the nostril

**SWELLING**
Abscess
Fracture
Hernia
Tumour

THIRST, EXCESSIVE
  Chronic nephritis
  Diabetes

URINE, BLOODSTAINED
  Cystitis
  Stones or gravel in the bladder

URINE, FREQUENT PASSAGE OF
  Chronic nephritis
  Diabetes
  Cystitis
  Partial blockage of the bladder

URINE, STOPPAGE OF
  Stones or gravel in the bladder

VOMITING
  Dietetic error including over-eating
  Roundworm infestation
  Furball
  Feline infectious enteritis
  Gastritis
  Foreign body in stomach or intestine
  Coccidiosis
  Poisoning
  Nephritis

## A–Z of ailments

### ABSCESSES

The formation of an abscess is a common sequel to a scrap with another cat or a bite from a rodent. The reason for this is that the teeth or claws of these animals inflict a small puncture wound and as the cat's skin is so elastic the hole closes very quickly, allowing any pus-forming bacteria which may have been introduced to multiply under the skin. The commonest sites are: at the base of the tail; the head; the limbs. The first sign is a swelling which quickly increases in size. The cat's temperature generally rises and as it does so the cat becomes listless, shows pain when the swelling is touched and probably goes off its food. Antibiotics administered in the early stages may disperse the abscess but if not it should be encouraged to come to a head as quickly as possible by the use of hot fomentations. Squeeze out a towel or sponge of hand-hot water and apply to the affected part, renewing the application several times and repeating the performance three or four times daily. If the abscess is on a paw or lower part of a leg, the limb can be immersed in a jug or jam jar of warm water.

When the abscess bursts, the larger the wound the better, otherwise it will heal over too quickly and more pus will be formed. Keep it open as long as possible by bathing with warm water containing a mild antiseptic and apply an antibiotic dressing. Quite often an abscess has to be lanced in order to give relief to the patient, or the wound enlarged to allow proper drainage.

A neglected abscess can lead to formation of fistulae and a chronic septic condition which is difficult to clear up.

Another common site for abscess formation is at the root of a rotten tooth. If this is not attended to, the bone of the jaw or a sinus will become infected. This should always be treated by your veterinary surgeon.

Neglected cases of ear-mite infestation can lead to pus forming in the ear or in the ear flap by the cat scratching and producing a self-inflicted wound which then becomes infected.

### ACID MILK

If the queen is ill, or has a digestive upset after kittening, her milk may become too acid. This will cause the kittens to be restless and cry a lot and in severe cases they may even die. When kittens do not appear to be thriving, have the mother's milk tested. If not too far advanced, the condition can easily be rectified by treating the mother for whatever is the cause of the acid milk. The kittens should be bottle-fed until the mother's milk is normal again.

### ALLERGIES

Cats suffer from allergies just as much as do other animals and the causes are just as varied. Some of the more common ones are:

*Fleas*—many cats are allergic to flea bites and suffer from 'flea eczema', a condition of the skin seen as widely distributed, small, itchy scars surrounded by sparse and broken hair.

*Plants*—sniffing certain plants produces sneezing, perhaps conjunctivitis and even asthma.

*Food*—as with people, cats can be allergic to various foods, notably fish and milk. The allergy is often seen as an eczematous condition of the skin.

*Drugs*—a cat can have an allergy to particular drugs.

The treatment of an allergy is naturally to remove the cause, at which the symptoms will rapidly subside. The difficulty is to pin-point the cause and in this case the owner's observation of the cat is essential. For instance, is it always after it has eaten a certain food or been seen at a particular spot in the garden that the cat shows allergic symptoms? However, when the cause is unknown anti-histamine drugs and sedative treatment will help.

### ANAL GLANDS

These are situated one either side of the anus and are small sacs which secrete a strong-smelling sebaceous fluid. Each sac has a tiny orifice and this can become occluded, causing the sac to become distended with fluid and sometimes infected so that an abscess forms. Unlike dogs, cats are seldom troubled by impaction of the anal glands and this may be because cats, by their frequent licking, prevent the orifices from becoming blocked.

The signs of anal-gland trouble are that the cat will be constantly licking the area and dragging its seat along the ground.

Treatment consists of emptying the glands by applying pressure and dealing with any infection by the use of antibiotics.

If the trouble is severe and of frequent occurrence, the glands can be removed surgically. This is hardly ever necessary in the case of cats.

### BRONCHITIS

This is usually encountered in the course of viral respiratory diseases but occasionally cats develop bronchitis from no known cause.

In the acute form the symptoms are: coughing, rise of temperature and lassitude. As well as veterinary treatment, nursing is most important. Keep the cat in a warm but well-ventilated room, feed a light, tempting diet and encourage the cat to take fluids. If breathing is difficult inhalations of Friar's Balsam will help.

The chronic form occurs usually after several acute attacks. The cat has a chronic cough—sometimes coughing up phlegm —loses condition and its appetite is variable.

COCCIDIOSIS

It is mostly kittens, even quite young ones, that are affected, although adult cats may carry the parasite without showing any clinical signs.

Coccidia are unicellular parasites which in the cat attack the lining of the intestine, where they can cause severe damage. They multiply in the bowel and their eggs are passed out in the faeces. Outside the host's body the eggs form spores and await ingestion either by the same kitten or another.

The symptoms are: frequent watery diarrhoea, sometimes bloodstained, small amounts produced with much straining; occasional vomiting, especially when the stomach is empty; loss of appetite; rapid loss of condition. Most textbooks say that coccidiosis in cats is rare but this has not been my experience. Perhaps the area in which I practised was particularly congenial to coccidia.

While medical treatment is necessary, it is just as essential to take strict sanitary precautions. Isolate infected kittens; use newspaper for bedding, change it daily and dispose of it by burning; use disposable feed dishes and burn them or use metal dishes and boil them once daily; use disposable sanitary trays and burn after use, or scrub metal or plastic trays with hot water containing household ammonia (two fluid ounces per gallon). The quarters should also be cleaned frequently with water and ammonia and allowed to dry thoroughly before returning the kittens to them. Clean up and burn faeces as often as possible. Contaminated runs should be dug over, treated with lime and not used for six months.

CONJUNCTIVITIS

Conjunctivitis is inflammation of the membrane lining the eye. It can arise from an irritant substance in the eye, or by blockage of the lacrimal duct, or as a symptom in the viral respiratory diseases. It can affect one or both eyes. Firstly the conjunctiva appears swollen and inflamed, then there is a watery discharge from the eye, which may become thick and yellowish in colour if pus-forming bacteria become involved.

In the early stages, bathe the eyes gently with warm boracic solution to remove any irritant substances. Use cotton-wool swabs soaked in the solution, a fresh swab for each eye. If the cat is not better within 24 hours, take to your veterinary surgeon, or earlier if there are any other symptoms, such as sneezing.

CONSTIPATION

This occurs in the course of some illnesses but in longhaired cats it is most often caused by swallowing loose fur. The mass of fur may be so large and felted by the time it reaches the rectum that the cat is unable to pass it. Matters are made worse by the cat straining to get rid of the furball and thereby squeezing out the fluid part of it. Dosing with liquid paraffin (mineral oil) may be sufficient to dislodge the mass but more probably an oily enema will be required.

A word of warning here. A cat affected by blockage of the bladder, whether partial or complete, behaves just like a cat suffering from constipation—squatting frequently in its sanitary tray, squeezing out drops of liquid faeces and probably drops of urine also. So before treating the cat for constipation please make sure that its bladder is not blocked. This can be done by *gently* palpating the abdomen. If you feel something hard and round, the shape and size of a cricket ball, the cat needs veterinary attention immediately.

Old cats are liable to suffer from constipation and this can often be corrected by adjustment of the diet, as discussed in the section on care of the old cat.

CYSTITIS AND URINARY CALCULI

Cystitis simply means inflammation of the bladder and may occur during some infections, owing to imbalance of the diet—particularly the fluid intake—but by far the commonest cause is the presence of calculi in the bladder and urethra. In the female, the calculi take the form of stones and surgical removal is necessary. In the male, stones are rare and the calculi appear as fine gravel or sand. What causes these calculi to form is a hotly debated subject and veterinary opinion is divided. It may be that there is more than one cause.

The first sign of cystitis is that the cat is seen frequently scratching about and squatting in its sanitary tray. It may pass small quantities of urine, or none at all if urinary calculi are causing a complete blockage of the urethra. Because of this behaviour the owner is often misled into thinking the cat is constipated and, consequently, treatment of the real cause is delayed, sometimes until it is too late. The cat is restless and, being in a considerable amount of discomfort and even pain, is unable to settle anywhere. It will often give cries of distress, especially when straining to pass urine.

Do not postpone calling your veterinary surgeon if you have any reason to suspect a urinary disorder. If calculi are present and are causing complete obstruction it is quite possible for the bladder to rupture. Therefore be careful how you handle a cat in this condition. The size of the bladder in individual cats varies, so that some cats will be *in extremis* more quickly than others. Treatment must be left to the veterinary surgeon in charge of the case. When calculi are present, surgery may be necessary and after treatment will include the use of drugs and special diets to prevent further formation of stones.

### DIABETES

This disease is seldom found in cats and then usually in middle-aged to elderly animals. The first signs are that the cat is drinking and eating more than normal but at the same time is losing weight. It also passes large quantities of pale urine. These symptoms also occur in chronic nephritis and a differential diagnosis has to be made by analysis of the urine. Treatment must be under veterinary supervision and is usually by daily injections of insulin. After the dose has been stabilized, the owner can give the injections.

### DIARRHOEA

It is quite natural for cats to pass soft, or even semi-fluid, faeces but with diarrhoea the bowel motion is completely fluid and more frequent than normal.

Diarrhoea is not a disease in itself; it occurs in the course of various diseases or it may be caused by internal parasites, tumours or poisons. However, the most common cause of diarrhoea is dietetic error, so first check your cat's diet for a possible source of trouble. Experience will tell you what will affect the individual cat—liver, for instance, will upset some cats' digestions—and you will soon get to know what is likely to be the cause in your own cats. If the cat seems well apart from the diarrhoea, try giving some kaolin powder in a tasty gravy and withhold food for 12 hours but if the animal is showing other symptoms, or if the diarrhoea does not clear up within a day or so, consult your veterinary surgeon.

Diarrhoea can be very tiresome in longhaired cats because of the soiling of their fur. You will in all probability have to wash the anal region, using mild soap (not detergent) and water, rinsing well and drying. Sprinkle on some talcum powder to control the odour. In severe cases, for the cat's comfort it may be better to clip the fur in the area. If the anus is inflamed, apply a little vaseline. In summer especially strict hygiene is necessary because blowflies lay their eggs on the soiled fur and when these hatch the maggots burrow into the cat's skin causing toxaemia and possibly death unless disposed of quickly.

### DISLOCATIONS

By far the commonest site is the hip joint, usually as the result of being hit by a car. The dislocation is reduced under a general anaesthetic and, provided that the ligaments are not too badly torn and the cat is immobilized for a few days at least, the outcome is usually good. Even if the bone does not stay in the socket, a false joint will eventually be formed and the cat be able to get around very well although the affected leg may be slightly shorter.

### EAR MITES

The parasite involved is otodectes cynotis. It is found in both cats and dogs and is one of the few diseases common to both. Therefore, if you own a dog and your cat is affected, be sure to examine the dog's ears and *vice versa*.

The mites live free in the ear canal causing intense irritation by piercing the skin to suck. An exudate is thus produced and is seen as the familiar reddish-brown ear wax. Through an auroscope the mites can be seen on this wax as tiny white moving dots. Whatever treatment is adopted, it is essential that the discharge should be cleared out before applying any drops or ointment. This can be done by swabbing the ear gently with cotton wool soaked in olive oil. Cotton-wool buds commonly used for babies' ears are suitable. There are proprietary brands of ear drops etc. in the market but unless the condition clears up quickly with these, it is better to get veterinary treatment.

### ECLAMPSIA

This is known as milk fever or lactation tetany because it occurs in the lactating female, usually within a few days after the kittens' birth, occasionally just before. It is caused by a drop in the blood calcium and this is one of the reasons why it is so important to give the pregnant queen supplementary calcium and Vitamin D. The latter is necessary for absorption of calcium. It is fairly uncommon in cats but, when a case does occur, veterinary assistance is required immediately. The queen will need an injection of calcium and probably also some sedation.

Symptoms include: panting, staggering, muscular twitchings, abrupt rise of body temperature, semiconsciousness, fits—death follows if the condition is untreated.

### ENTROPION

This means inversion of the eyelids. It is usually the lower lid that turns in but the upper one can also be affected, especially at the outer corner. The condition used to be fairly common in longhaired cats but is seldom seen now, which is a good thing because it is painful for the cat and requires surgical correction. The bone structure of the longhaired cat's face predisposes to the condition but it can also be hereditary, therefore affected cats should not be used for breeding.

The signs are that the cat blinks the affected eye and often half closes it; at the same time there is a discharge of tears and often a dark-brown crust along the inturning lid. Irritation is caused by the hairs on the eyelid rubbing on the cornea.

FELINE INFECTIOUS ENTERITIS (also called panleucopaenia)

This disease is caused by a virus and it can be rapidly fatal, especially in kittens and young cats. Before vaccination against the disease was available it was very common in all cats— whether pets or those kept in catteries—and it really was a nightmare for those wishing to exhibit cats. Very often kittens would become infected at shows and, apart from developing the disease themselves, brought home the infection to the cattery. The development of safe and efficient vaccination is about the best thing that has happened in the cat world, because epidemics of the disease are now rare. Antibiotics and other modern drugs, by controlling secondary infections, have reduced the fatality rate.

The symptoms are: vomiting, lassitude, rise of temperature and rapid deterioration in condition. If a kitten is vomiting and looks very poorly, get veterinary help as quickly as possible.

FLEAS

The presence of fleas is naturally more of a problem in long-hairs than in short-coated cats, the long coat being the ideal home for the flea. If the cats are confined to a cattery, it is reasonably easy both to prevent infestation and to clear it up should it occur. But cats which have free range are liable to become re-infested, so that de-fleaing becomes a matter of routine. Use a reliable brand of insecticide, suitable for cats. Avoid those containing chlorinated hydrocarbons such as DDT and BHC.

Most longhair cats give very little sign of having fleas, apart from scratching and licking. Some do not even do that. The typical 'flea eczema' is generally seen in shorthaired cats. The presence of fleas can be confirmed by finding what looks like black grit in the coat. This is flea excreta. Affected cats should be treated once weekly, the insecticide powder being sprinkled into the coat, making sure it gets right down to the roots. Leave for ten minutes or so then brush out the excess powder. At the same time the cat's bed and bedding must be treated. Fleas

M

lay their eggs in dry, dusty places, especially between floor-boards so all possible breeding places should be treated with powder or a liquid insecticide. It is also possible to catch and kill the fleas on the cat by using a fine-tooth comb. Anti-flea collars are not suitable for use on longhaired cats.

FRACTURES

In the adult cat, fractures are almost always the result of a road accident and the most common sites are the femur, the pelvis and the lower jaw. Limbs may also be fractured if the cat falls from a height. The tail may appear to be fractured by being shut in a door but this is usually a displacement rather than fracture of a vertebra.

Young kittens sustain fractures by being dropped, trodden on, or shut in doors and the type of fracture in this case is usually the end of a long bone becoming detached from the shaft.

If you suspect your cat has a broken leg, do not attempt to put a splint on it—you will do more harm than good because the cat is sure to struggle. Immobilize the cat and the best way to do this is to lift it carefully and put it in a basket or box until it can have veterinary attention.

Broken legs in longhaired cats generally heal very well because of their sturdy rounded bones which contain plenty of bone marrow. Fractures are mostly repaired by pinning or plating, sometimes by plaster-of-Paris bandage but you will in any case have to arrange to confine the cat for some time until healing has taken place.

HAEMATOMA

When a cat is constantly shaking its head or scratching its ear due to the presence of ear mites then it is very liable to produce a haematoma. This is a swelling of the ear flap and is caused by the rupture of a blood vessel with the consequence that the flap fills with blood or blood serum.

The swelling may be small to start with, but if not treated fairly quickly the whole flap will soon be involved. Surgery will more than likely be necessary in any case. If the condition is not treated, the cat will certainly be left with a crumpled ear but in any case there may be some crumpling, depending on the amount of damage to the cartilage of the ear.

Until you can obtain veterinary help, try to prevent the cat from shaking its ear. This can best be done by pulling a section of an old stocking over the head and making a small hole for the sound ear to go through which will then anchor the stocking.

### HAIRBALL

A hairball, or furball, occurs when the loose dead hair which a cat swallows while grooming itself accumulates in the stomach or intestine and forms into a round or sausage-shaped mass. If a large quantity of fur is involved, the mass may become felted and so solid that the cat is unable either to vomit it or pass it in its bowel motion. In this case an operation to remove the hairball may be necessary. Fortunately this very rarely occurs. But longhaired cats can hardly avoid swallowing some fur, which they get rid of either by vomiting or in the faeces. Very often the cat will eat coarse grass to act as an emetic and so help it to get rid of the fur. Sometimes the cat will be sluggish, lack appetite or even be completely off its food.

Prevention of hairball is of course better than cure and regular grooming will help, especially during the moulting season. Skin diseases and parasites such as fleas produce irritation, resulting in excessive licking, so keep the cat's skin healthy and free from parasites.

During the moult give a small dose of liquid paraffin or olive oil to act as a bowel lubricant or a bulk laxative can be mixed in the food. Never give castor oil, which purges violently.

### HARVEST MITES

As the name implies, these mites are seen in late summer. You may be lucky enough to live in an area where they never appear but in other places they crop up every year. The mites attach themselves to the skin, not to the hair, so that short-haired cats are more likely to become infested than are long-hairs. They look like a cluster of tiny orange-coloured specks and are found in and around the ears, on the thin skin between the toes and the sheath of skin around the claws. They cause some irritation.

Treatment is either by insecticide powder or by sponging affected parts with a mild disinfectant in water.

### HERNIA

The type of hernia most likely to concern the cat owner is the umbilical hernia. It happens when the abdominal muscles fail to close at the umbilicus, with the result that either abdominal fat or a portion of intestine protrudes through the hole. The hernia under the skin is first seen or felt in the kitten as a soft non-painful swelling, most obvious when the kitten is standing, sometimes disappearing altogether when the animal lies on its back. It is advisable to have veterinary advice on a hernia. If the hole in the muscle is small, so that only a little fat can pass through it, the condition is not likely to cause trouble and quite often the small hole closes as the kitten gets bigger. But if the hole is large enough for a loop of intestine to slip through, it is possible that the bowel could distend with gases and become strangulated. If this should happen an immediate operation is required.

### JAUNDICE

This is not a disease in itself but is a symptom of various diseases in which the liver is involved, or in some cases of poisoning. Veterinary treatment is indicated. All fats or fatty foods should be withheld and the cat encouraged to drink water containing glucose.

### LICE

These are very seldom seen on cats and they are difficult to see when they are present. They are so small that they look like flakes of dandruff until they are seen to move.

Treatment is the same as for fleas but repeat the powdering two or three times at intervals of 5–7 days, because the egg of the louse (nit) is fixed to the cat's fur and will not be destroyed until it has hatched.

### MAGGOTS

These are sometimes found in longhaired cats. If there is a small abscess or wound which is covered by the hair, or where the fur round the anus has been soiled by diarrhoea, this is an ideal place for the blowfly to lay its eggs, especially if the cat is ill or aged and so unable to repel the fly. The eggs then hatch into maggots which burrow under the victim's skin and will cause its death by toxaemia if not destroyed.

Clip the fur from the affected part, dispose of all maggots, clean up the area with mild antiseptic and apply antibiotic ointment or talcum powder.

### MASTITIS

This occurs during lactation and especially when the queen has only one or two kittens to feed but has produced a large quantity of milk. The kittens do not draw off the milk from all the mammary glands and so one or more of the glands becomes impacted and is hard, swollen and hot to the touch. Apply hot fomentations and gently milk the gland until it is soft and supple again. If neglected a breast abscess may develop. This will require antibiotic treatment and may have to be lanced.

### NAILS

Apart from in tiny kittens and elderly cats, nails seldom require attention if the cat is able to sharpen them on trees or a scratching post. Of course, if these are not available your furniture will do just as well, a habit better discouraged from an early age.

Small kittens sometimes get their nails caught in their mother's fur, or may scratch her when they are sucking. Carefully snip the very tips of the nails with a sharp pair of clippers or scissors.

Old cats usually need a regular manicure and you can do this yourself with a pair of nail clippers, taking care to cut just the tip of the nail. If you cut into the quick you will cause the cat pain and the nail will bleed. Even cutting too near the quick, thereby compressing it, will cause the cat discomfort. Better to cut just a little and do it more often. The best method is to get someone to hold the cat while you grasp one paw and by gently squeezing a toe between your finger and thumb the nail will extrude and can be easily snipped. Repeat all round.

NEPHRITIS (or inflammation of the kidneys)

Acute nephritis is uncommon but may be caused by poisons which affect the kidneys or occur in the course of an illness such as feline infectious enteritis. The cat will refuse all food, vomits, appears very unwell, has pain in the lumbar area and is usually very thirsty.

Chronic nephritis is frequently seen in older cats. If there is not too much damage to the kidney tissue it is possible to keep the disease under control by diet and drugs. The symptoms are: excessive thirst, loss of weight and passage of large quantities of urine. Veterinary diagnosis and treatment is essential for both forms of nephritis.

PLEURISY AND PNEUMONIA

There are various causes of these conditions but they are probably most frequently seen as complications of the viral respiratory diseases. Diagnosis and treatment must be left to the veterinary surgeon.

RESPIRATORY DISEASES (viral)

Known to most people simply as 'cat flu', the viral respiratory diseases are the most infectious of all cat ailments.

Symptoms depend on the type of virus involved and include: sneezing, watery discharge from the eyes and nose, ulcers on the tongue, gums, and hard palate, coughing, and a rise of body temperature. In some cases the lungs are affected and this is usually the most serious type.

As well as veterinary treatment, good nursing is of great importance, as discussed earlier.

The whole cattery must be placed in quarantine until given a clearance certificate by the veterinary surgeon in attendance. As well as the cats, the humans also should not come in contact with other cats.

The most likely places for your cat to become infected are at cat shows and in a boarding cattery and this is not in any sense a criticism of these places. Despite all precautions, a cat which is incubating the disease or a carrier cat may be present. Both at shows and while boarding, your cat may be under a certain amount of stress and is then more likely to succumb to infection. A cat which is not 100% fit is more likely to develop the disease and to be more badly affected, so never take your cat to a show or send it to board unless it is in the best of health.

The skin trouble most commonly seen in longhair cats is a dry eczema, often called miliary eczema, taking the form of tiny scabs. These usually first appear on the back and sides and spread to the rest of the body. The hair becomes dry, broken and sparse. The cat licks and scratches the affected parts, often producing a wet eczema which appears as a swollen, pink, wet patch.

The causes of eczema are many and include external parasites, hormone imbalance, allergy and dietetic errors. Modern methods of treatment are usually very successful but this is a condition which tends to recur.

*Alopecia* is loss of hair without any lesions on the skin and is mostly seen in neuter cats. The hair usually disappears on the abdomen and the inside of the thighs. Some cats respond well to hormone treatment, others do not.

*Mange* in the cat is caused by the mite *notoedres cati* which affects the head, making the skin appear wrinkled and causing the hair to fall out. It is very seldom seen nowadays, is relatively easy to treat and there is little risk of humans becoming infected.

*Ringworm* is a disease of the skin or the hair, depending on which type of this parasitic fungus is the cause of the trouble. If the skin is affected, bald circular patches will be seen, or sometimes just scabby areas. When the hairs are affected, the appearance may just be that of a very scurfy coat—often likened to cigarette ash. Positive diagnosis is made microscopically and by culture of material from the lesions. Treatment is simpler than it used to be and both internal and external methods are used. But still the owners must be very careful when handling an infected cat as this is the disease which is most likely to be transmitted to man. The cat should be confined in one easily cleaned place until it is free from infection, isolated from other cats and also from children who are highly susceptible to ringworm. When handling the cat wear rubber gloves, burn soiled bedding and litter and use disposable dishes and litter trays.

## SNAKEBITE

In this country the only poisonous snake is the adder. Cats are not often bitten, probably because of the speed of their reflexes. If they should be bitten it is usually on the forepaw or leg. The wound appears as two small bleeding holes and the area around is swollen. The cat appears shocked. Put the cat in a basket or container to avoid movement, keep it warm and get veterinary treatment as soon as possible.

## STINGS

Longhaired cats are rarely stung on the body because of the protection their fur gives them but bee or wasp hunting quite often leads to a sting on the lips or forepaw. If you see the sting, (it looks like a thorn) remove it with tweezers and apply a paste of bicarbonate of soda and water to the swelling.

## STROKE

This is essentially a complaint of the older cat and is not usually fatal but the severity of the stroke or number of recurrences may lead to euthanasia.

The symptoms appear suddenly and include staggering, loss of balance, holding the head on one side, dilation of one pupil and contraction of the other, the eyes oscillating, paralysis of one or more limbs.

Rest and sedation are the main lines of treatment. The cat should be confined to a basket as soon as symptoms appear, otherwise it may damage itself in staggering about and in its distress may provoke another stroke.

If the cat has difficulty in eating and drinking because of loss of balance, it will have to be hand-fed until it has compensated.

Another problem may be difficulty in balancing while in the sanitary tray and in this case the cat should be supported by a hand placed firmly on either side of its body.

## TEETH

Baby or 'milk' teeth appear at 3–4 weeks of age. These are

shed at about 3–4 months and the permanent teeth, 30 in number, are usually all present by the time the kitten is six months old.

Kittens seldom have teething troubles in the way that puppies do. Sometimes they have a slight tummy upset when the permanent teeth are erupting. A few drops of milk of magnesia daily in the food will help at this time.

Cats' teeth are very brittle and fracture easily in an accident. The broken teeth should be extracted, otherwise the roots readily become infected.

Teeth should be inspected regularly because cats so often accumulate a deposit of tartar on the teeth. This looks something like the fur inside a kettle in a hard-water area. The tartar should be removed because it causes the gums to recede, allowing the entrance of bacteria. This can be done by use of a tooth scaler but if there is a lot of deposit it may be necessary for the cat to have a general anaesthetic.

The deposit of tartar can be prevented to a certain extent by regularly giving the cat hard food to chew or a large bone to gnaw (no splintery bones or any small enough to be swallowed).

TICKS

Cats may pick up sheep or cattle ticks from long grass. The tick, which is a small, greyish-brown, oval object, buries its head in the animal's skin in order to suck blood. As it engorges with blood so its body enlarges and when full it drops off the host.

Treatment with insecticide powder may cause the tick to drop off, or it can be removed with tweezers, but you must then be very careful that the head is not left embedded in the cat's skin. A dab with surgical spirit will make the tick relax its hold but be sure to have someone to hold the cat firmly because the spirit stings the raw spot where the tick is embedded.

TUMOURS

They are fairly common in the older cat and are often malignant.

The malignant lymphosarcoma is found in the internal organs, particularly the kidneys and intestines.

Carcinoma particulary affects the skin of the head region, occurring mainly in the ears, eyelids and lips. It is also commonly found on the tongue.

Osteosarcomata (bone tumours) are usually found on the skull and long bones.

Mammary tumours, especially carcinomata, are one of the most common in the cat.

Papillomata are found in the external ear canal and tend to set up an otitis but otherwise are of no great importance.

The only method of treatment of malignant tumours is surgical but this must be carried out in the early stages and even then the chances of regrowth and spread are great.

## WORMS

### Hookworms

These are rarely seen in the cat in Britain, but are found in the United States and in hot climates. The larvae of the hookworm thrive in moist conditions and are not resistant to sunlight, so in the event of an infection in a cattery keep the premises dry and airy.

### Roundworms

Roundworms found in the stomach of the cat cause little or no trouble to the host, which usually gets rid of them by vomiting. Worms found in the intestine, while not affecting the adult cat, may cause mild to severe illness in kittens. Although not likely by themselves to be fatal to the kitten, they can produce such debility that the kitten succumbs to a bacterial infection.

Symptoms of roundworm infestation in kittens are: sickness, diarrhoea—sometimes bloodstained—harsh coat, coughing, lack of condition and 'pot'-belly. The worms may be passed in the bowel motions.

A positive diagnosis can be made by microscopical examination of the faeces. Treatment is simple nowadays: no starving is necessary and the kittens are seldom upset by the dose. The appropriate tablet will be supplied by your veterinary surgeon.

As the larvae of one type of roundworm can affect man and particularly children, it is a sensible precaution to worm all kittens at 5–6 weeks of age and to keep the kittens and their sanitary trays scrupulously clean. This applies to puppy roundworms too.

*Tapeworms*

The head of the tapeworm is attached to the intestinal lining and from the other end of the worm ripe segments containing the eggs are shed and passed with the cat's faeces. They may be seen on the fur around the anus. When fresh they are creamy-white, resembling flattened grains of rice, becoming brittle and straw-coloured after an hour or two. The eggs must pass through an intermediate host, most frequently the flea, but rabbits and mice can also be involved, depending on the type of tapeworm. The cat becomes infected by eating the intermediate host.

Because the tapeworm is attached to the bowel wall, treatment is not quite as simple as for roundworms and should always be under veterinary supervision. It is essential to rid the cat of any fleas it may carry, otherwise it will become re-infested.

# Index